LATHE

{ the tool information you need at your fingertips }

skills institute
press

Distributed By
Fox Chapel Publishing

FOX CHAPEL
PUBLISHING

© 2010 by Skills Institute Press LLC
"Missing Shop Manual" series trademark of Skills Institute Press
Published and distributed in North America by Fox Chapel Publishing Company, Inc.

Lathe is an original work, first published in 2010.

Portions of text and art previously published by and reproduced under license with Direct Holdings Americas Inc.

ISBN 978-1-56523-470-3

Library of Congress Cataloging-in-Publication Data

Lathe.

    p. cm. -- (The missing shop manual)

Includes index.

ISBN: 978-1-56523-470-3

1. Lathes.

TJ1218.L347 2010
684'.08--dc22

                            2009037801

To learn more about the other great books from Fox Chapel Publishing,
or to find a retailer near you, call toll-free 800-457-9112
or visit us at *www.FoxChapelPublishing.com*.

Note to Authors: We are always looking for talented authors to write new books
in our area of woodworking, design, and related crafts.
Please send a brief letter describing your idea to Acquisition Editor,
1970 Broad Street, East Petersburg, PA 17520.

Printed in China
First printing: February 2010

Contents

WHAT YOU WILL LEARN

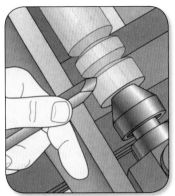

Chapter 1
The Wood Lathe, page 6

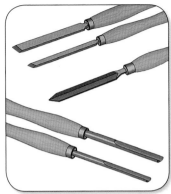

Chapter 2
Turning Tools, page 22

Chapter 3
Lathe Setup, page 28

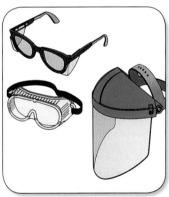

Chapter 4
Safety, page 48

Chapter 5
Sharpening, page 52

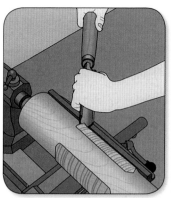

Chapter 6
Spindle Turning, page 74

Chapter 7
Finishing Spindles, page 102

Chapter 8:
Faceplate Turning, page 108

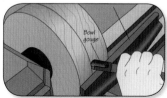

Chapter 9:
Bowl Turning, page 128

CHAPTER 1:
The Wood Lathe

The wood lathe is the oldest of all woodworking machines. Primitive forms of the lathe were used by the Etruscans in the ninth century B.C. Throughout its long history, the tool has been used in virtually the same way. Somewhat like a potter's wheel laid on its side, the lathe spins a wood blank while a turner shapes the wood with chisel-like tools. The lathe makes it possible to shape wood into flowing, rounded forms in a way that other tools cannot.

The earliest lathes were human-powered, with a piece of cord wrapped around the blank, connected to a springy sapling and a treadle. With a few modifications, this evolved into the pole lathe popular with British bodgers, who traveled from town to town, working freshly fallen trees into chairs. Flywheels and driveshafts were added to the design, and the lathe emerged as one of the engines behind the mass production of Windsor chairs in the mid-eighteenth century. Turning became a specialized trade.

Turned legs and other furniture parts are shaped on the lathe in a process called spindle turning. Above, a wood blank is mounted between the lathe's fixed headstock in the upper left-hand corner and the adjustable tailstock near the center of the photo. The tailstock slides along the lathe bed to accommodate the workpiece. The blank is turned into a cylinder and then shaped with a variety of sharp turning tools.

Turning blanks are typically available in short pieces. Some of the more popular examples are shown here. Resting atop a zebrawood board are samples of tulipwood, kingwood, and ebony. For a selection of the best woods for turning, see page 15.

With the coming of the Industrial Revolution, heavy cast engine-powered lathes forever took the elbow grease out of turning. With minor changes, the lathes were essentially the same as those used by modern woodworkers. Indeed, many wood turners prefer older lathes to newer ones, refurbishing them and setting them on stands of their own making. Woodworkers were beneficiaries of technological advances in machining made during the Industrial Revolution when lathes were adapted to turn metals, as well as wood. This new field brought the wood turner a wide range of chucks and accessories to hold the most delicate and tricky of turned objects, from goblets to lace bobbins.

The lathe is one of the most popular woodworking tools, and wood turning is a craft with an intriguing cachet, like carving or marquetry. It is not hard to understand why: A lathe enables the woodworker to turn something beautiful from nothing more than a stick of wood—and in a short time.

CHOOSING A LATHE

When you choose a lathe, consider carefully the type of turning you will be doing. Some models are made specifically for faceplate turning, in which the blank is secured only on the head-stock. Others are small enough to rest on a benchtop. The lathe shown on page 10 is a typical freestanding model used for both spindle and faceplate turning.

Lathe size is measured in two ways: swing and capacity. Swing is twice the distance between the headstock spindle and the bed, which limits the diameter of blanks. Capacity is the distance between the headstock and tailstock, which limits the length of blanks. The weight of the lathe is important, as greater weight provides stability and dampens vibration. Another feature to consider is how easy it is to change speeds; larger workpieces must be turned at lower speeds than smaller ones. Changing the speed of some lathes involves switching a drive belt between two sets of stepped pulleys. Other models have variable-speed pulley systems that allow the speed to be changed without switching off the motor.

If you decide to buy a used lathe, check the motor, bearings, spindle threads, and lathe bed for wear. Make sure the tool rest and tailstock run smoothly and all locking levers work. Also make sure that the spindle thread is standard. If not, chucks and other accessories must be rethreaded to fit.

ANATOMY OF A LATHE

Faceplate Standard lathe attachment; blank is fastened to faceplate which is then threaded onto headstock spindle.

Tool rest Provides support and fulcrum point for tools when turning. Height of rest can be adjusted and locked in place with lever; rest can be rotated to the desired angle for faceplate turning.

Headstock Holds blanks for both faceplate and spindle work; central shaft that turns spindle is attached to motor via drive belt. Removable cover allows access to drive belt and indexing head.

Tool base Slides along lathe bed between headstock and tailstock to position tool rest.

On/off switch

Variable speed control lever Increases or decreases speed of spindle rotation without shutting off the lathe; pulled out and turned to change speed.

Locking lever Locks tailstock in place.

Spindle lock Locks tailstock spindle in place.

Tailstock spindle A hollow shaft with a reverse taper that holds centers in a friction fit to turn spindle work; turning tailstock handwheel advances and retracts spindle.

Tailstock handwheel Advances and retracts tailstock spindle to secure workpiece.

Tailstock Secures one end of blank for spindle turning. Slides along bed to accommodate blanks of different lengths.

Bed Made of two cast-iron or tubular steel tracks, or ways, typically spaced 1½ inches apart; accurately machined so that the tool base and tailstock slide smoothly.

HEADSTOCK

Indexing head Enables spindle to be rotated a preset number of degrees by hand when carving flutes, reeds, and spiral turnings on a blank. Features one ring of 60 holes spaced 6° apart around the head and another of 8 holes spaced 45° apart; indexing pin is inserted in a hole when carving is being done and taken out to rotate spindle. Lathe must be switched off during entire operation.

Spindle nut Loosens to remove spindle for replacing belts and bearings

Headstock spindle Threaded hollow shaft to which various chucks are screwed in place; ranges from ½ inch to 1½ inches in diameter. Hollow is Morse-tapered to hold various centers with a friction fit.

Fixed width pulley Features four adjustable steps. On lathes with variable-speed adjustment, spindle speed is changed by manually moving belt from one step to another; on variable-speed models, belt is left as is.

Indexing pin Fits into holes in indexing head; inserted to hold headstock spindle steady and retracted to rotate spindle by hand.

DRIVE

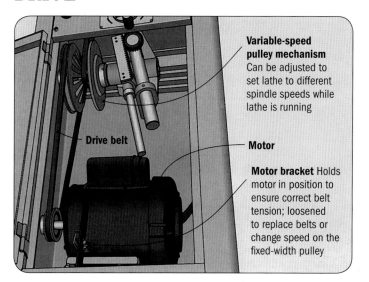

Variable-speed pulley mechanism Can be adjusted to set lathe to different spindle speeds while lathe is running

Drive belt

Motor

Motor bracket Holds motor in position to ensure correct belt tension; loosened to replace belts or change speed on the fixed-width pulley

The 1950s-vintage Wadkin Bursgreen lathe is prized for its machining capacities and innovative features, such as a brake that stops spinning blanks quickly and a removable bed segment near the headstock to accommodate large-diameter faceplate work.

WOOD FOR TURNING

In some ways, selecting wood for turning is like choosing lumber for any woodworking project. Stock should be free from defects, such as knots, splits, checks, and shakes. Blanks for spindle turning should be straight-grained; for bowls and other faceplate work, grain is less of a concern. In fact, a wildly figured piece of wood can yield a stunning bowl.

In other ways, selecting wood for turning has some advantages: Because wood turners are not limited to boards and planks, small offcuts at the lumberyard or fallen fruit trees at a local orchard can provide the needed raw materials.

Turning is typically done with hardwoods, as softwoods are often incapable of rendering sharp detail. Exotic woods are popular with many turners because of their striking figure; however, many are being harvested at an alarming rate and some are scarce and very expensive. Check with your local dealer for exotics from well-managed sources. See the list at right for the characteristics and uses of some common turning woods.

While it is preferable to turn wood that has been air- or kiln-dried to a moisture content of 8 to 10 percent, green wood can also be used. Blanks for large, deep bowls are sometimes best cut from a freshly felled tree. While green wood is easier to turn, it shrinks more, and some distortion is to be expected.

WOOD FOR TURNING *(continued)*

Wood for Turning

WOOD TYPE	CHARACTERISTICS AND USES	PRICE AND AVAILABILITY
Apple	Hard, tough wood with attractive straight grain and fine, even texture; light sapwood, reddish-brownish heartwood. Good workability; accepts finishes well. Excellent for small, ornate turnings.	Moderate; relatively plentiful
Cocobolo	A heavy, dense tropical exotic with medium texture and straight to irregular grain; purple, orange, rust and yellow in color with black markings. Moderate workability; finishes well and takes a high polish yet produces noxious dust when sanded. Used for small spindle turning projects such as vases, cutlery, and tool handles.	Expensive; scarce
Mahogany	Straight to interlocked grain, moderately coarse texture, light reddish-brown to medium red. Good to excellent workability, depending on species; takes finishes very well; a tough, strong wood for general turning.	Moderate; becoming scarce
Maple	Straight grain, occasionally curly or bird's-eye, fine texture; reddish-brown heartwood and white sapwood. Good to moderate workability; accepts finishes very well. Hard and dense, maple is suitable for general and fine turning.	Inexpensive to moderate, depending on figure; plentiful
Olivewood	Interlocked grain with fine, even texture; yellowish-brown with variegated streaks. Moderate to difficult workability; accepts finishes very well and takes an unusually high polish. Ideal for ornate turning.	Expensive; rare
Pear	Straight grain; fine, even texture; pinkish-brown to reddish-brown. Excellent workability; takes a high polish. Typically used for fine, ornate turning, and musical instruments.	Expensive; rare
Rosewood	Straight to interlocked grain, depending on the species; golden-brown to dark, purple brown. Good workability; accepts finishes well, provided the species is not too oily. Used for fine turning.	Expensive; becoming scarce
Tulipwood	Irregular grain, medium-fine texture; rich golden-pinkish hue with salmon to red stripes. Difficult workability; splits easily. Accepts finishes very well; can be brought to an unusually high polish, yet produces noxious dust when sanded. Used for small, ornate turnings.	Very expensive; scarce

BASIC TURNING TOOLS

Parting tool
Narrow cutting tool used for making
sizing cuts and forming tenons;
available in ⅛ and 3⁄16 inch widths.

Roughing gouge
Cutting tool used to rough out
cylinders from square stock; available
in widths between ¾ and 1½ inches.

Skew chisel
Angled cutting tool used for making
beads, V-cuts, and shoulder cuts and
for smoothing surfaces; available in
widths between ½ and 1¼ inches.

Spindle gouge
Used for cutting beads and coves and
for general spindle work; available in
widths between ¼ and ½ inch.

TURNING A SPINDLE

Marking Centers

To mount a blank between centers on the lathe, mark two lines across each end from corner to corner. The lines will intersect at the center. Next, use an awl to make indentations at both points (right).

Mounting the Blank

Butt one end of the blank against the tailstock's live center. Supporting the other end of the blank with one hand, slide the tailstock toward the headstock until the drive center in the headstock aligns with the indentation you just made. Secure the tailstock in place with the locking lever and advance the tailstock spindle and center by turning the handwheel until the blank is held firmly between the centers (below). Secure the tailstock spindle in place with the spindle lock.

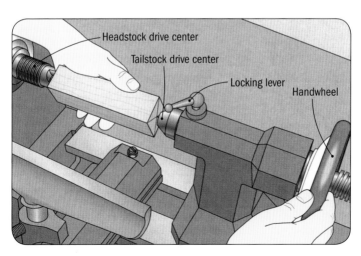

Headstock drive center

Tailstock drive center

Locking lever

Handwheel

TURNING A SPINDLE *(continued)*

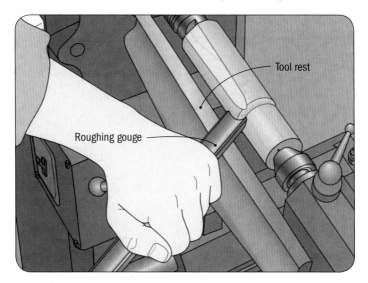

Tool rest

Roughing gouge

Roughing Down

Holding a roughing gouge with a overhand grip, brace the blade on the tool rest. Cut very lightly into the blank, making sure the bevel is rubbing against the stock and moving the gouge smoothly along the tool rest. The gouge will begin rounding the corners of the workpiece. The smoothest cuts are made by moving the blade with the grain. Continue making successively deeper passes along the blank, raising the handle of the tool with each pass, until the edges are completely rounded and you have a cylinder (above). Adjust the position of the tool rest as you progress to keep it as close to the blank as possible.

TURNING A SPINDLE *(continued)*

Coves

Outline the cove on the blank with a pencil. Then, hold a spindle gouge in an underhand grip with the flute pointing sideways and slice into the wood just inside one of the

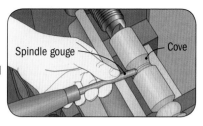

marked lines with only the cutting edge of the tool. Slowly angle the tool handle back toward the line until the bevel rubs on the workpiece, and make a scooping cut down to the middle of the cove. As you make the cut, turn the handle to rotate the bevel against the workpiece. The gouge should be flat on its back when it reaches the center of the cove. Make the second cut from the opposite side of the cove. Work in a downhill direction, from a high point to a low point on the blank so the tool does not dig into the wood (above).

Beads

A skew chisel enables you to turn beads with sharp detail. Outline the bead on the stock with a pencil, then make a V-cut at each line. For best results, use the long point of the chisel. Then, working on one side of the V-cuts, widen the cut, slowly lifting the handle so the bevel rubs and the long point of the chisel makes a rounded, rolling

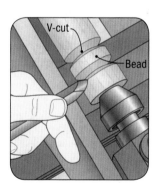

cut (right). Repeat for the other side of the bead, making sure your cuts are always made in a downhill direction. Once the shape of the bead is smooth, turn a round shoulder on each side of the bead.

TURNING A BOWL

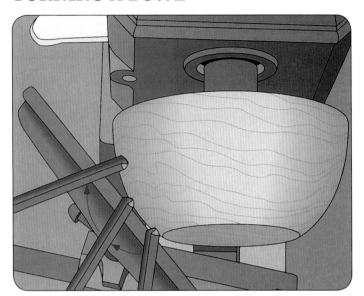

Rounding the Blank

Rotate the blank by hand, ensuring it does not contact the rest. Bracing the gouge on the tool rest at one edge of the piece, advance the blade until the heel bevel contacts the stock. Pivot the handle until the cutting edge slices into the wood. Move the tool along the blank to remove a thin layer of wood.

Rounding the Outside

Work from center toward the rim of the blank to shape the outside of the bowl. As shown above, you will need to pivot the handle and roll the blade to keep the bevel rubbing on the stock. Refine the shape of the bowl with the bowl gouge, adding designs as desired. Remember to account for the method you will use to chuck the bottom of the bowl to the headstock to hollow out the inside.

TURNING A BOWL *(continued)*

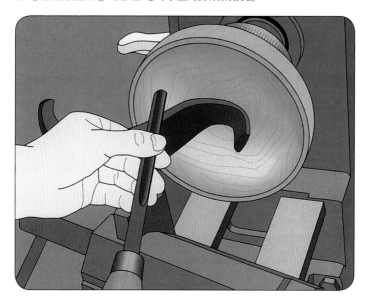

Hollowing the Inside

Flatten the face of the bowl and then make a depth hole to ensure
the bowl is hollowed to the correct depth. Then position the tool rest
so the gouge tip will cut slightly above the middle of the blank. Turn on
the lathe and align the cutting edge just to the left of the center of the
blank. With the gouge on its side and flute facing forward, push the tool
slowly into the blank. Turn the inside to match the outside, leaving the
walls a bit thicker than you want them. Smoothing (p. 142), scraping
(p. 144), and Finishing (p. 147) will follow to achieve your
desired results.

Turning Tools

Unlike other stationary machines, the lathe is not equipped with blades or bits.

Instead, you need to buy a set of turning tools to do your work. These tools resemble wood chisels, except they are tempered and shaped differently, with longer handles and blades for better control and leverage.

Turning tools can be divided into two basic groups: cutting and scraping tools. Cutting tools are most often used in spindle turning, where the grain of the wood runs parallel to the lathe's axis of rotation. These tools include gouges, chisels, and parting tools. Scraping tools are usually used in faceplate turning, where the grain runs perpendicular to the axis of rotation.

Traditionally, all turning tools were made of carbon steel, but this material has a tendency to overheat during grinding and with continuous use. Turning tools made of high-speed steel (HSS) retain their edge up to six times longer than carbon steel, making the additional expense worth it in the long run. In fact, some tools, like deep-fluted bowl gouges and large scrapers, are only available in HSS. Whether they are made from high-speed or carbon steel, turning tools should always be kept sharp, using techniques described in Chapter 5, which begins on page 52. A blunt tool is an accident waiting to happen.

SCRAPING TOOLS

Square-end scraper
Used for flattening and smoothing convex faceplate work such as the outside of bowls; cutting edge beveled on the underside at 80°. Available in widths between ¼ and 1 inch.

Round-nose scraper
General-purpose scraping tool for smoothing and finishing concave surfaces in faceplate work such as bowls or hollow vessels; available in widths from ½ to 1 inch.

Side-cutting scrapers
Specialized ¾-inch scrapers used on the inside of bowls and other hollow faceplate work.

Half-round scraper
Larger 1½-inch version of round-nose scraper for heavy-duty bowl work; comes in left-and right-handed models.

Skew scrapers
Angled 1½-inch square-end scraper for rounding convex surfaces and marking concentric cuts in faceplate work; comes in left-and right-handed models.

Domed scraper
Version of round-nose scraper for making fine shearing cuts and finishing inside of bowls and other hollow faceplate work; available in widths between ½ to 1 inch.

CUTTING TOOLS

Skew chisel
Angled cutting tool used for making beads, V-cuts, and shoulder cuts and for smoothing surfaces; beveled at 42° on both top and bottom. Available in widths between ½ and 1¼ inches.

Fluted parting tool
Parting tool with cove along the bottom; tapers from ³⁄₁₆ to ⅛ inch at the top of blade. Two leading spurs at the bottom score outline of cut first, reducing friction and binding.

Radiused skew
A straight skew given a curved edge on the grinder; enables complex smoothing cuts to be made without digging into the work.

Oval skew
Features a rounded body for making beads or pommels; easier to control than a straight skew. Available in ¾- and 1-inch widths.

Standard parting tool
Narrow cutting tool used for making sizing cuts; beveled on top and bottom at 50°. Available in ⅛- and ³⁄₁₆-inch widths.

Diamond-section parting tool
Diamond-shaped parting tool that tapers from ³⁄₁₆ inch wide at center of blade to ⅛ inch wide at the edges, enabling it to cut with less friction than standard parting tool.

CUTTING TOOLS *(continued)*

Bowl gouge
Deeper-fluted version of the spindle gouge; used in shaping bowls, cups, and other faceplate work. Available in widths between ¼ and ½ inch.

Roughing gouge
Cutting tool used to rough out cylinders from square stock for spindle work; beveled at 30°. Available in widths between ¾ and 1½ inches.

Spindle gouge
Shallower than bowl gouges with a fingernail grind beveled at 30°; used for cutting beads and coves and for general spindle work. Available in widths between ¼ and ½ inch.

Deep-flute bowl gouge
A bowl gouge with a deeper flute used in roughing and finishing bowls, vessels, and other faceplate work. Available in widths between ¼ and ¾ inch.

Beading tool
Square chisel used to produce beads and V-grooves; beveled at 60°. Available in ¼- and ⅜-inch widths.

Square-end chisel
Similar to a skew chisel but ground straight across; available in ½- and 1-inch widths.

SPECIALTY TOOLS

In their quest for better tools, some woodturners design their own. California engineer and woodturner Jerry Glaser developed a line of turning tools using A-11 high-speed steel, some of which are shown in the photo at left. The hollow aluminum handles are filled with lead shot to dampen vibration and give the proper weight to the tool. Some of the handles and blades are interchangeable.

Hook tool
Patterned after specialty Swedish woodturning tools; used in end-grain hollowing. The short hook is for hollow work with gradual interior curves; the long hook is for forms with tight internal curves, such as a necked vase. Sold without handles.

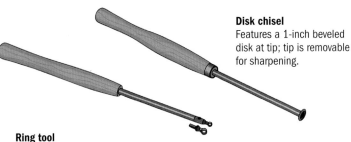

Disk chisel
Features a 1-inch beveled disk at tip; tip is removable for sharpening.

Ring tool
Used for end-grain hollowing of vases, boxes, and other hollow turnings; ideal for areas difficult to reach with a bowl gouge. Interchangeable cutting rings are sharpened on the inside bevel; removed and installed with a setscrew. Rings are $5/16$, $7/16$ and $9/16$ inch in diameter.

BEGINNER'S KIT

There is a bewildering variety of turning tools on the market, yet only eight to ten are needed to undertake most common turning. A beginner's tool kit is outlined below, at right.

- A **1-inch roughing gouge** for rapid removal of stock between centers.

- **2 skew chisels**: a ¾- or 1-inch tool for planing and tapering, and a ½-inch tool for finer work such as shaping curves and making decorative cuts.

- **2 spindle gouges**: a ¾- or 1-inch tool for general spindle turning, and a ½-inch tool for finer spindle work.

- A **¼-inch diamond section parting tool** for parting off and making sizing cuts.

- A **⅜-inch bowl gouge** for faceplate turning of bowls up to 10 inches in diameter.

- A **¼-inch deep flute bowl gouge** for faceplate turning.

- A **¾-inch round nose scraper** for cleaning up concave surfaces and hollow faceplate work.

- A **1-inch square-end scraper** for flattening and smoothing convex surfaces.

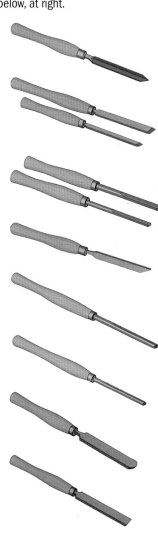

CHAPTER 3:
Lathe Setup

A tool rest acts as a fulcrum for your turning tools, providing a fixed, horizontal, weight-bearing surface for balancing and bracing a tool as you cut into a spinning blank. The tool rest on a lathe is made up of two parts: a tool base and the detachable rest itself. The base can slide along the length of the lathe bed, according to the needs of the work. The tool rest mounts in the base; the height and angle of the rest are adjustable so it can be positioned parallel to the lathe bed for spindle and faceplate work, perpendicular to the bed for faceplate work, or at an angle in between. In addition, the base and rest can be mounted on an outboard bed for large-diameter faceplate turning. There are a number of different tool rests for specialized turning tasks; a selection is shown at right.

Standard tool rest
Mounts in tool base for general faceplate and spindle work; comes with lathe.

TOOL RESTS

Standard tool base
Slides along the lathe bed; features a fitting for tool rest shaft. A lever-operated cam mechanism locks base in position on the bed. Base shown is the type that comes with most lathes.

Long rest
Mounted in two standard tool bases for long spindle work; available In 18- and 24-inch lengths.

Tall tool base
Used on lathes with lower outboard beds for turning large faceplate work, this base is 4 inches taller than standard bases; a lever-operated cam mechanism is used to lock the base in position.

S-shaped bowl rest
Used for turning the outside and inside of bowls.

Right-angle rest
Mounted in standard tool rest to turn bowl blanks.
Long side is perpendicular to lathe bed to turn face of bowl. Short side parallel to lathe bed to work sides. Long side typically 7 inches.

Short rest
Used for smaller spindle and faceplate work; typically 6 inches long.

DRESSING A TOOL REST

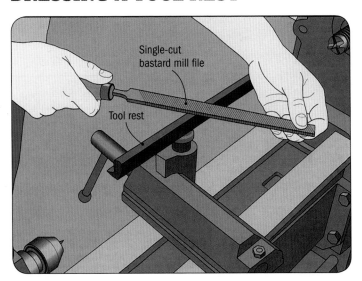

Single-cut
bastard mill file

Tool rest

Because a tool rest is made of softer steel than the steel used for
turning tools, it will eventually develop low spots, marks, and nicks.
If not remedied, these imperfections will be transferred to the blanks
you turn, or make the tool you are holding skip and possibly cause an
accident. You can dress a tool rest easily with a single-cut bastard mill
file. Holding the file in both hands at an angle to the rest, push it across
the top surface. Make a series of overlapping strokes until you remove
all the nicks and hollows from the rest, then smooth the surface with
200-grit sandpaper or emery cloth followed by a light application of
floor wax, buffed smooth.

LATHE CENTERS

Two-spur drive center
Mounted in headstock spindle to center and drive spindle work; point centers the workpiece while chisel-like spurs engage and turn it. Features Morse taper shaft; useful with blanks with ends that are not square.

Live center
Mounted in tailstock spindle to center workpiece; features Morse taper shaft. Large hub contains bearings, allowing center to spin with the work, eliminating friction.

Four-spur drive center
Mounted in headstock spindle to center and drive spindle work; features Morse taper shaft. Offers better grip and drive on square-cut work than two-spur center.

Cone center
Used with a live center to support hollow workpieces held at the headstock end only; cone has several steps of decreasing diameters.

Dead center
Mounted in tailstock spindle to center and drive spindle work; features Morse taper shaft. Remains fixed with respect to spinning work; some lubrication is needed. Model shown is a cup center, featuring raised ring to prevent splitting of small work.

Lace-bobbin center
Mounted in headstock to turn small work such as bobbins; features Morse taper shaft. Tapered square hole will hold stock $5/16$- to $1/2$-inch square.

DRIVE CENTERS

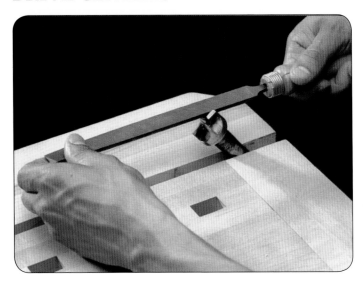

The drive centers of a lathe should be kept as sharp as your turning tools. If the spurs or point of a drive center are dull or chipped, they will not grip the workpiece properly. Sharpen drive centers on a bench grinder or with a file (above). A 35° bevel on the underside of each spur works best.

After sharpening the drive spurs, remove the centerpoint with a hex key and sharpen it to a uniform taper. Replace the point in the center so it protrudes ⅛ inch beyond the spurs, and tighten it with the key.

LATHE BED

Center Alignment

Turning between centers requires precise alignment of drive centers between headstock and tailstock, otherwise you will produce off-center turnings. To see if the drive centers line up, insert a four-spur drive center in the headstock and a live center

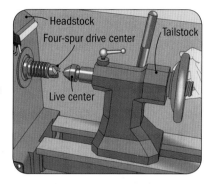

in the tailstock (right). Slide the tailstock along the bed up to the drive center. The points of the drive centers should meet exactly. If they do not, you may have to shim the tailstock or file down its base.

Smooth Ways

If your shop is in a humid climate, the bed of your lathe may develop a thin layer of rust that can prevent the tailstock and tool rest from sliding smoothly. To keep the lathe bed clean, remove any rust as soon as it appears by sanding the bed with fine sandpaper (below), 200-grit or finer, then apply a paste wax.

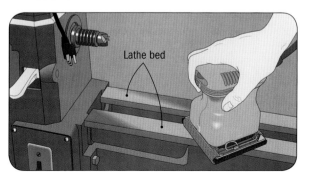

CHANGING SPEED

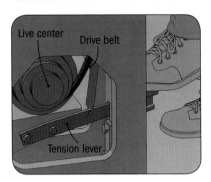

To change the speed on a lathe that features stepped pulleys, unplug the machine and lift open the headstock cover. Step on the tension lever to disengage the ratchet and raise the motor, releasing the drive belt tension and loosening the belt.

Adjusting Height

The height of a lathe is crucial to efficient turning. Commercial lathe stands are often too low, which can make it difficult to control your turning tools. You also may tire more as a result. As a rule of thumb, the height of a lathe's spindles should be level with your elbows. If necessary, you can raise your lathe to the proper height by bolting it to solid blocks of dense hardwood with foam rubber glued to their undersides.

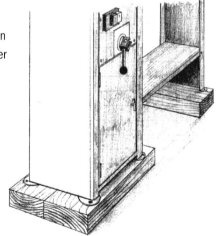

CHANGING SPEED *(continued)*

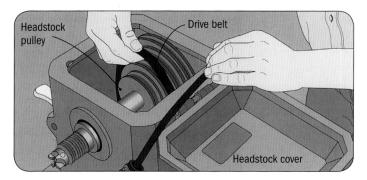

Headstock pulley — Drive belt — Headstock cover

To set the desired speed, follow the manufacturer's instructions for adjusting the position of the belt. (On the model shown, these instructions are printed on a nameplate on the underside of the headstock cover.) Refer to the chart below to help you select the right speed for the blank you plan to turn. Position the drive belt on the appropriate step on the motor pulley and then align it with the correct step on the headstock pulley. Once the drive belt is in position, step on the tension lever again to lower the motor and tighten the belt. Close the headstock cover.

Lathe Speed Chart

FACEPLATE TURNING SPEEDS		
Diameter	**Up to 2" thick**	**Over 2"thick**
Up to 8"	1250 RPM	1000 RPM
8-12"	1000 RPM	750 RPM
12-18"	750 RPM	300 RPM
More than 18"	300 RPM	slowest speed

SPINDLE TURNING SPEEDS			
Thickness	**Up to 12" long**	**12-24" long**	**Over 24" long**
Up to 2½	2500 RPM	1750 RPM	1250 RPM
2½-4	1750 RPM	1250 RPM	1000 RPM
More than 4"	1250 RPM	750 RPM	slowest

LATHE STAND

Older lathes are prized by wood turners because they were often built better than newer models. The only problem is that these vintage lathes often lack a stand or a working motor. Fortunately, it is easy to equip a lathe with both. Lathes need less powerful motors than most stationary machines. A ½-hp model that runs at 1725 rpm—half the speed of a table saw motor—will do.

A lathe stand needs to be heavy and solid, like the rugged shop-built version shown below, constructed primarily from 2-by-6s. The motor is mounted behind the lathe, with the pulleys under a safety guard. The stand also features a wooden tension pedal that allows you to release belt tension and stop the spindle instantly. Refer to the illustration for suggested dimensions.

For the stand, start by cutting the legs to length from four 2-by-6s, then saw a triangular notch from the bottom of each leg to make feet. Join each pair of legs with two crosspieces, locating one crosspiece just above the feet and the other 1½ inches from the top of the legs. Cut the shelf from two 2-by-6s, and screw the pieces to the lower leg crosspieces.

Shop**Tip**

Adding Weight
Because turning wood can cause a great deal of vibration, a lathe needs to be as stable as possible. Since most modern lathe stands are made of lightweight steel, it is necessary to weigh them down with cement blocks or sacks filled with sand, as shown here, to reduce vibration and noise.

LATHE STAND *(continued)*

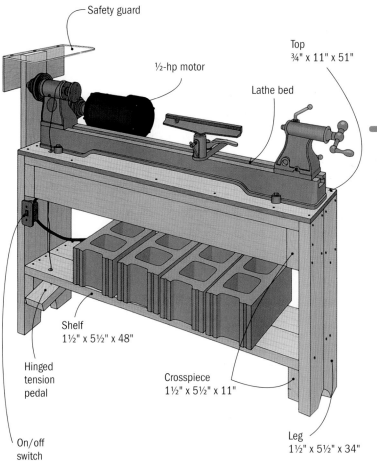

Safety guard

½-hp motor

Top
¾" x 11" x 51"

Lathe bed

Shelf
1½" x 5½" x 48"

Hinged
tension
pedal

Crosspiece
1½" x 5½" x 11"

On/off
switch

Leg
1½" x 5½" x 34"

LATHE STAND *(continued)*

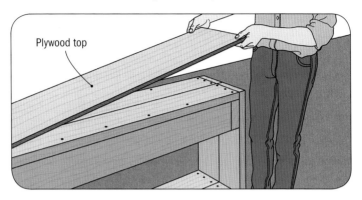

Plywood top

Next, install the top, cut from two 2-by-6s and a piece of ¾-inch plywood. Screw the boards and two braces to the upper leg crosspieces, then fasten the plywood to the 2-by-6s, as shown above. Bolt the lathe to the top of the stand.

Screw the motor to a mounting board cut from ¾-inch plywood. Then fasten the board to the top with butt hinges so the steps in the motor pulley are in line with the headstock pulley steps (below). Mount the drive belt on the pulleys.

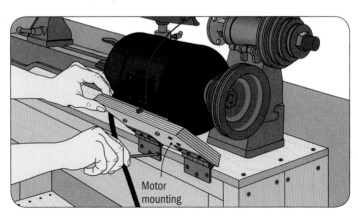

Motor mounting

LATHE STAND *(continued)*

Next, make and install the tension pedal. Connected by a length of wire to the motor-mounting plate, this wooden pedal will allow you to slacken the drive belt with simple foot pressure, disengaging the motor from the headstock and stopping spindle rotation. Cut the pedal from 2-by-4 stock so it will extend out from under the shelf by about 4 inches when it is installed. Attach the tension pedal with

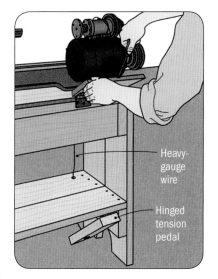

Heavy-gauge wire

Hinged tension pedal

another hinge to the underside of the shelf, directly under the motor. Bore holes through the top, the shelf, and the pedal to accommodate the wire that will connect the pedal to the motor-mounting board. Attach a length of heavy gauge wire to the underside of the pedal and pass it through the three holes you drilled and over the headstock. Now push the motor-mounting board toward the lathe and hold the wire against it. Keeping the tension pedal flat on the floor, pull the wire taut. Cut the wire and screw it to the back of the motor mounting board (above). Release the motor; the tension pedal should rise from the floor. To check the pedal, step on it; the wire should pull the motor-mounting board and motor towards the lathe, releasing the tension on the belt. Lastly, install an on/off switch for the motor at the front of the lathe stand, and place concrete blocks or other heavy objects on the shelf to weigh down the stand and reduce vibration.

CHUCKS

Mounting stock in a lathe requires several basic accessories. If you are turning between centers, or spindle turning, you will need a variety of centers that fit in the headstock and tailstock of the machine (page 31). As the blank turns, the centers grip it at both ends.

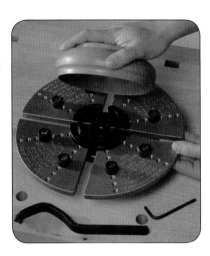

Faceplate turnings, such as bowls or plates, can be screwed to a simple faceplate and threaded onto the headstock. Smaller or more delicate turnings, such as lace bobbins, should be held by a chuck.

There is a range of lathe chucks, each serving a different purpose, from the simple screw chuck to the scroll chuck. The latter comes from the field of metalwork and features three or four jaws that open or close around the workpiece. Some chucks are designed as combination chucks, and comprise a number of parts that can be reconfigured to hold stock in several ways.

Arbor screw chuck
Used to mount faceplate work to the headstock; mounts in pilot hole drilled in workpiece. Includes a 2½-inch backing washer for large work; some models feature adjustable screws.

Three-way split ring chuck
Used to mount long hollow turnings such as goblets and vases to the headstock; beveled rings fit into sizing cut made in a workpiece and lock against the beveled internal face of chuck collar. Part of combination chuck system.

CHUCKS *(continued)*

Spigot chuck
Used to mount faceplate work to the headstock; chuck collar tightens spigot jaw around either dovetail or parallel spigots turned in the base of workpiece. Part of combination chuck system.

Dovetail chuck
Used to mount bowls and other faceplate work to the headstock; as screw collar is tightened with wrenches shown, beveled jaws expand against a dovetailed recess turned in the base of your workpiece. Part of combination chuck system.

Jacobs chuck
Three-jaw chuck used to hold small turning work in the headstock or boring attachments in the tailstock; features Morse taper shaft.

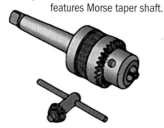

Pin chuck
Used when roughing out large faceplate blanks mounted to the headstock; inserted into hole bored in workpiece. Part of combination chuck system.

Four-jaw scroll chuck
Another combination chuck system that can be used as a dovetail, spigot, pin, or screw chuck; jaws expand and contract on slides as chuck scroll is rotated with wrenches shown. Larger jaws can be added.

RACK FOR TOOLS

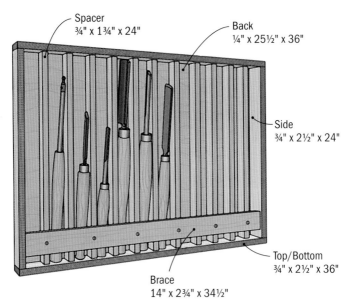

Spacer
¾" x 1¾" x 24"

Back
¼" x 25½" x 36"

Side
¾" x 2½" x 24"

Top/Bottom
¾" x 2½" x 36"

Brace
14" x 2¾" x 34½"

Keep your turning tools organized and within reach with one of these shop-built racks. They are simple to make; adapt the dimensions in the illustrations to accommodate your tool collection. The rack shown above is made from ¼- and ¾-inch plywood and features spacers to separate the tools and a brace that prevents them from falling forward. To make the rack, cut the back, top, bottom, and sides of the frame and screw the pieces together. Mount the spacers to the back with a screw at the top and bottom, spacing the strips every 2½ inches. Finally, position the brace about 1 inch from the bottom of the rack and screw it to every second spacer.

RACK FOR TOOLS *(continued)*

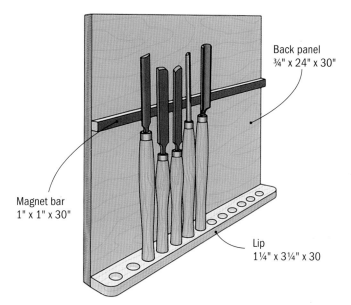

Back panel
¾" x 24" x 30"

Magnet bar
1" x 1" x 30"

Lip
1¼" x 3¼" x 30

The rack shown above relies on a magnetic bar to hold tools upright. Instead of a frame, this rack features a ¾-inch plywood backing panel. Cut the lip from solid wood and bore a row of 2-inch-diameter holes to accommodate the handles of your turning tools; drill each hole halfway through the lip and space them 2½ inches apart. Attach the lip flush with the bottom of the panel, driving screws from the back. To position the magnetic bar, set a few of your tools upright in the rack—including the shortest one—and mark a line across the panel at the level of the blades. Screw a 1-inch-square strip of wood to the panel over the line and glue a magnetic strip to the wood.

MEASURING TOOLS

Despite its visual appeal and emphasis on "feel" as a method of judging the progress of a workpiece, woodturning is an exacting craft. To obtain the required precision, the headstock of your machine must run smoothly and true, and the workpiece must be carefully centered.

Experienced turners worry less about centering than beginners. They know how to quickly reduce the rough blank to an accurate cylinder on the lathe.

The tools illustrated below and on page 45 will help you to set up your lathe and accurately measure the progress of your work. Use them well; it is difficult to judge a bowl's depth by eye or duplicate the contours of a turned leg without a set of calipers.

The commercial center finder shown at bottom left of page 45 takes the guesswork out of mounting spindle stock to the lathe. The jig is useful for round and octagonal stock, and for remounting work once the waste ends have been cut away. The blank is held in the bottom of the jig, rapped with a mallet, rotated a quarter turn, and then hit again. The two lines scored on the end will indicate the center of the piece. For added convenience, mount the jig on a wall.

Combination calipers
Feature a set of inside calipers at one end and a set of outside calipers at the other. Useful for sizing lids to fit turned boxes. Available in 6- to 12-inch spans.

Inside calipers
Used to determine inside diameter of hollow turnings; available in 4-, 6-, and 8-inch spans.

MEASURING TOOLS *(continued)*

Double-ended calipers
Feature a set of outside calipers at each end. A dimension taken at one end is automatically transferred to the other; calipers do not have to be removed from workpiece to take measurement. Available in 8- and 10-inch spans.

Outside calipers
Used to determine thickness of spindle or faceplate work; available in 4-, 6-, and 8-inch spans.

Compass
Used to scribe a circle on a blank; typical span is 6 to 8 inches.

Dial calipers
Usually used to measure diameter and wall thickness; makes precise inside and outside measurements. Graduated in $\frac{1}{1000}$-inch increments.

Sizing tool
Attached to a beading or parting tool, as shown, for producing accurate diameters in spindle work. Knob opposite cutting edge rests against spinning blank as cutter reduces thickness.

Center finder
Quickly locates center of square, round, or octagonal spindle stock up to 6 inches wide; features steel scoring blade to mark stock.

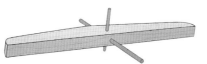

Depth gauge
A shop-made gauge consisting of a wood handle and two dowels used to determine the depth of bowls and hollow turnings; the longer dowel features depth increments. Model shown can measure bowls up to 17 inches in diameter.

CHECKING BEARINGS

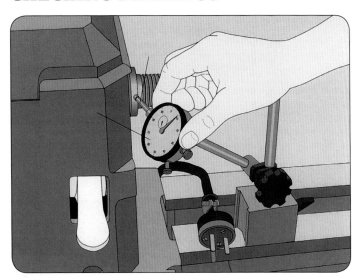

If your lathe is an older model, check the bearings periodically for runout—the amount of wobble in the spindle. Clamp a dial indicator to a magnetic base and position it with its plunger touching the lathe's spindle (above), then calibrate the dial to zero following the manufacturer's instructions. Turn the shaft of the lathe by hand; the dial indicator will register bearing runout. If the runout exceeds 0.005 inch, the bearings should be replaced.

DUST HOOD

Turning can generate a great volume of waste wood and dust. Built entirely from ¾-inch plywood, the dust hood shown at right can be positioned directly behind a workpiece to draw chips, shavings, and sawdust from your lathe and convey this debris to your dust collector. Refer to the illustration for suggested dimensions. Make the stand high enough for the hood to sit at the level of the workpiece when the base is on the shop floor.

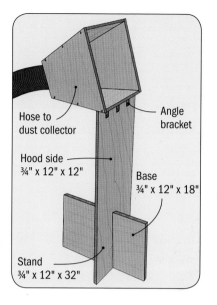

Hose to dust collector

Angle bracket

Hood side
¾" x 12" x 12"

Base
¾" x 12" x 18"

Stand
¾" x 12" x 32"

To build the jig, cut the base and stand, and connect them with an edge half-lap joint. Next, cut the four sides of the hood, starting with 12-inch-square pieces and tapering each to 6 inches at the back. Use glue and screws to connect the pieces. Cut a panel to fit the opening at the back of the hood, beveling its edges so that it fits snugly. Use a saber saw to cut a hole for a dust collection hose, then glue and screw the back panel to the hood. Attach the hood to the stand with three angle brackets on each side of the stand. The front of the hood should protrude over the edge of the stand to balance the assembly.

To use the jig, insert a dust collector hose into the back panel. Place the dust hood directly behind the workpiece and turn on the dust collector before you start turning. You can install casters at the bottom of the base and stand, if desired.

CHAPTER 4:
Safety

Although turning is considered to be a relatively safe pursuit, it is not free of danger. Getting your fingers pinched between a spinning blank and a tool rest is only one hazard. Most turning accidents can be attributed to mounting a blank on the lathe improperly, or using inappropriate speed or tool technique. Carefully center a blank on the spindle and check that you are using the proper speed for the job before you start turning. The speed must be compatible with the size and weight of the workpiece; see page 35 for a chart indicating the appropriate speeds for various turning operations. Finally, never use a cutting tool for something it was not designed to do, and make sure your tools are sharp.

The safety accessories shown on page 49 are as important as sharp tools. Because of the large amount of chips and dust produced by turning, eye and face protection are essential. Wood dust packs some hidden hazards as well. Exotic woods, such as rosewood and tulipwood, produce toxic dust that can cause serious eye, throat, and skin irritation. Wear a dust mask or respirator when turning any wood and equip your shop with an adequate dust collection system. A shopmade dust hood for the lathe is shown on page 47.

Reusable dust mask

Features a neoprene rubber or soft plastic frame with an adjustable head strap and a replaceable cotton fiber or gauze filter; protects against fine dust when sanding.

Safety goggles
Flexible, molded plastic goggles protect eyes from flying debris and sawdust.

Face shield
Clear plastic shield protects against flying debris; features adjustable head band.

Turner's smock
Three-quarter-length, wrap-around smock keeps loose clothing out of the way and free of dust.

Integrated respiration system
Features a helmet, protective face shield, strap-on filter, and battery pack; filter sends clean air up to helmet and face seal keeps dust out. Battery provides up to 8 hours of continuous use; filters last for several hundred hours.

Lathe shield
Protects lathe operator from debris; post is bolted to lathe bed. Large grill behind lathe contains debris; plastic panels in front allow operator to view work. Panels can be swung up out of the way for easy access.

SAFETY TIPS

- Do not wear loose clothes, neckties, or rings while turning; remember to roll up your sleeves.

- Wear appropriate safety equipment at all times.

- Make sure the lathe is properly grounded, and on its own electrical circuit.

- When finishing, do not use large cloths, as they may catch and pull your fingers into the work.

- Check the speed of your lathe before you turn it on; do not use excessive speeds.

- Ensure there is adequate lighting for your work. The lathe should have as much natural light as possible; place it by a window if your shop has one.

- When using the indexing pin, make sure the lathe is unplugged to prevent the spindle from rotating accidentally; be sure to disengage the pin before plugging in the lathe.

- Check for defects in the wood you are planning to turn; avoid blanks that have twists, splits, or knots.

- Always use the correct tool for the job.

- While turning, concentrate on the work at hand, and take frequent breaks to avoid fatigue.

SAFETY TIPS *(continued)*

- Always work with properly sharpened tools. Dull tools are more dangerous than sharp ones

- Keep the tool rest as close to the workpiece as possible without interfering with your ability to use your tools properly; rotate the work by hand first to see that it turns freely.

- Do not operate the lathe under the influence of alcohol or medication.

The hood worn by the turner is hooked to a small, belt-mounted pump and filter that provide fresh air. The clear plastic shield provides protection from flying debris.

CHAPTER 5:
Sharpening

Sharp tools are the cornerstone of wood turning. Dull cutting edges are not only more difficult and dangerous to use, they will also produce poor results. Take the necessary few minutes to sharpen your tools before you turn on your lathe.

The first step of sharpening involves grinding a tool's bevel to a suitable angle. There is some disagreement among turners as to what this angle should be for every tool. But as long as a bevel is either hollow-ground (concave) or flat, it will work well. As you gain experience, you may settle upon angles that suit your style of turning. Grinding is discussed on page 54.

Not surprisingly, there are several ways to sharpen turning tools. A few turners do all of their sharpening with benchstones and slipstones. Others sharpen exclusively on a grinding wheel. This is a quick and easy method of forming the edge you need, particularly midway through a turning project when you want to touch up an edge quickly. A wheel, however, may leave rough marks on the blade, preventing it from cutting cleanly and causing it to dull relatively quickly. As shown in this chapter, there is a good compromise: Start by rough-sharpening at the grinder and finish by honing the edge on a benchstone or slipstone. A bench grinder's felt wheel will perform the job of a slipstone, polishing the bevel to a razor-sharp edge (page 55). Scrapers differ from cutting tools because they depend on a burr instead of an edge for cutting. The burr can be made with a grinder, a bench stone, or a burnisher (page 72).

Once you have chosen a sharpening method, you will need to develop a technique. Seasoned turners sharpen freehand, but for the beginner, a commercial sharpening jig for use on a grinder is a worthwhile investment. There is a range of sharpening stones and wheels available. The inventory on page 56 and the chart of grinding wheels on page 57 should provide you with the information you need to make an informed purchase.

Like turning tools, grinders themselves require maintenance. Dressing the wheel occasionally (page 58) will ensure your tools are being sharpened by fresh abrasive particles. Check your wheels for cracks by tapping them: A wheel in good condition will produce a ringing sound. As an additional safety precaution, wear eye protection whenever you grind.

A wet/dry grinder is valuable for sharpening turning tools. Its wheel rotates more slowly than that of a conventional bench grinder, reducing the risk that the temper of the steel will be destroyed.

SHARPENING BASICS

Before you can sharpen a turning tool, the bevel angle must be ground properly. The grinding requirements of cutting and scraping tools are different because of the way they are used on the lathe. The bevel of a cutting tool must rub on the stock at all times

The grinder is a multipurpose tool for the wood turner. Here, the nicked cutting edge of a skew chisel is squared before grinding the bevel.

to help control the cut. If the angle is too sharp, the tool will be harder to control and the cutting edge will dull quickly. But if the bevel angle is too steep, you may have to hold the tool almost vertically and apply excessive pressure. Scrapers, on the other hand, shave away wood with a burr. The angles they require depend on the type of scraper you are using.

In addition to the bevel angle, the shape of the tip—straight across, skewed at an angle, or curved—is important to consider when grinding your tools. A square-ground spindle gouge, with a tip ground perpendicular to the blade shaft, is best for turning cylinders, tapers, or other straight cuts. A fingernail-ground spindle gouge, with edge corners cut back, or relieved, will make a better tool for turning beads and coves. Skew chisels may be ground straight across or curved, depending on the use. See page 60 for an illustration of the tips of various turning tools.

As you grind a bevel, it is critical to create a single-faceted bevel, that is, one with a continuous face. To create one, keep the bevel perfectly flat on the wheel as you grind. The jig shown on page 62 will help you with a troublesome tool, the roughing-out gouge. If you use a grinder, the bevel will have a shallow concave shape, matching the curve of the grinding wheel. Avoid using a wheel smaller than 5 inches in diameter; the degree of curvature will make for a weak tool tip. Grinding on a belt sander (page 64) will yield a flat bevel, which is equally effective.

SHARPENING EQUIPMENT

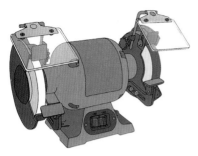

Dresser
Used to true or reshape grinder wheels and expose a fresh cutting surface. Star-wheel dresser (top) has up to four star-shaped wheels; diamond-point dresser (below, bottom) features a diamond set in a bronze tip on a metal shaft.

Bench grinder
Grinding or abrasive wheel (left-hand side) squares and sharpens blades; felt wheel (right-hand side) polishes the bevel near the cutting edge. Features ¼- to ½-hp motor; eye shields, adjustable tool rests, and wheel guards are standard on most models; bench-top grinders are usually bolted to a work surface.

Neoprene wheel
Rubber grinding/sharpening wheel; available in four grits. Used for grinding and sharpening; provides a sharp enough edge for turning without additional buffing or honing. Wheel must turn away from tool edge to prevent it from catching on the wheel surface.

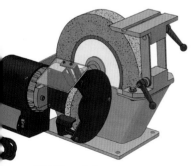

Aluminum-oxide wheels
Standard grinding wheels, available in 6- and 8-inch sizes and a range of grits.

Felt wheel
Available in soft, medium, or hard; dressed with buffing compound to perform final polishing of cutting edge.

Wet/dry grinder
Large 10-inch water-bathed wheel hones bevels; water prevents tools from overheating and carries away metal and grit. Five-inch dry wheel used for grinding. Each wheel equipped with an adjustable tool rest.

SHARPENING EQUIPMENT *(continued)*

Honing compound
Applied to cloth wheel of grinder to polish sharpened bevel; contains a mixture of chromium dioxide and other fine abrasives.

Slipstones
Small oilstones and waterstones used to hone bevels of turning tools; convex, concave, and conical stones are suited to curvatures of various gouges.

Benchstone
Any oilstone, water-stone, or diamondstone used to hone bevel of tools.

Adjustable tool rest and sharpening jig
Tool rest with tilting table (above, top) mounts to bench in front of grinder; table has slots for sliding tool guides and four settings on side bracket to adjust table to suitable angle for bowl gouges, spindle gouges, and skews. Available with accessory tool guides for gouges and skews (above, left) and for straight chisels and scrapers (above, right). Diamond-point wheel dresser (far right) rides in slot in table to dress grinder wheel.

Multi-tool jig
Adjustable tool rest (right) mounts to bench in front of grinder; features a 4-inch-wide table with a slot for sliding jigs and center-drilled for rotating jigs, Skew-grinding jig (above, top) holds skews at 20° angle, pivots on center pin to grind radiused skews, and folds out of the way for freehand grinding. Sliding sharpening jig (above, bottom) clamps tools under crossbar and slides in groove in table.

GRINDING WHEELS

The wheels supplied on grinders are usually too coarse for use with turning tools. A variety of replacement wheels are available, but selecting the right one is no simple matter. You need to decipher the codes marked on the side of the wheels, describing their composition and abrasive quality. The chart below will help you interpret these codes. (They are usually found sandwiched between two numerical manufacturer's symbols on the side of the stone.) If you plan to use a wheel to grind carbon steel tools, and then hone with a benchstone, buy a wheel marked A 80 H 8 V. This means the wheel is aluminum oxide (A), fine grained (80), and relatively soft (H), with a medium structure or concentration of abrasives (8). The particles are bonded together by a process of heat and fusion, known as vitrification (V). For high-speed steel tools, a medium hardness of I or J is better. If you plan to use your tools right off the grinder, choose a wheel with a grain size of 100 or 120.

Standard Marking System Chart			
Abrasive Type	**A:** Aluminum oxide **C:** Silicon carbide **Z:** Aluminum zirconium		
Abrasive (Grain) Size	**Course:** 8, 10, 12, 14, 16, 20, 24	**Medium:** 30, 36, 46, 54, 60	**Fine:** 70, 80, 90, 100, 120, 150, 180 **Very Fine:** 220, 240, 280, 320, 400, 500, 600
Grade Scale	**Soft** ———————→ **Medium** **Hard** A B C D E F G H I J K L M N O P Q R S T U V W X Y Z		
Structure	**Dense** **Open** 1 2 3 4 5 6 7 8 9 10 11 12 13 14 15 16 etc.		
Bond Type	**B:** Resinoid **BF:** Resinoid reinforced **E.** Shellac **O:** Oxychloride **R:** Rubber **RF:** Rubber reinforced **S:** Silicate **V:** Vitrified		

DRESSING A WHEEL

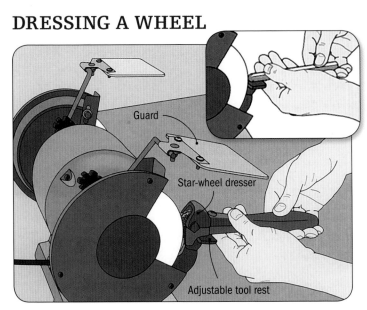

Guard

Star-wheel dresser

Adjustable tool rest

Using either a star-wheel or a diamond-point dresser, true a grinding wheel when ridges or hollows appear on the stone or it becomes discolored. For the star-wheel dresser above, move the grinder's tool rest away from the wheel. With the guard in position, switch on the grinder and butt the tip of the dresser against the wheel. Then, with your index finger resting against the tool rest, move the dresser from side to side. To use the diamond-point dresser (inset), hold the device between the index finger and thumb of one hand, set it on the tool rest, and advance it toward the wheel until your index finger contacts the tool rest. Slide the tip of the dresser across the wheel, pressing lightly while keeping your finger on the tool rest. For either dresser, continue until the edges of the wheel are square and you have exposed fresh abrasive.

GRINDING ANGLES

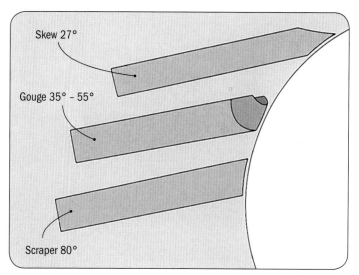

Skew 27°

Gouge 35° – 55°

Scraper 80°

The angle at which you present a tool to the grinder determines the angle of the bevel. The diagram above shows the angles at which gouges, scrapers, and skew chisels should be held to the grinding wheel to produce suitable bevels.

TOOL SHAPES

Skew chisel
Grind bevels so they meet at 40° to 50°; typically comes with cutting edge angled at 20° to 30°.

Ring tool
Comes pre-ground to correct bevel.

Round-nosed scraper
For shear scraping, grind bevel to 80°, leaving a burr on the edge; for general scraping, a 30° to 45° angle works better. Some turners use an angle of 75° to 80° for both types of scraping.

Bowl gouge
Grind bevel to 55° angle. A fingernail grind is shown here, with corners of cutting edge ground back from cutting edge to keep the tool from digging into stock; some turners use a straight-across grind.

Radiused skew
Has a slightly rounded cutting edge; grind bevels so they meet at 50° to 60°.

Spindle gouge
Grind bevel to 35° angle; can be given a fingernail or straight-across grind.

Roughing-out gouge
Grind bevel to 45° angle; cutting edge is ground straight across.

Parting tool
Grind bevels so they meet at 50°.

ROUGHING GOUGE

Restoring the Bevel

Position the guard and turn on the machine. Holding the blade between the fingers and thumb of one hand, set the cutting edge on the tool rest and advance it until the bevel lightly contacts the grinding wheel (right). If you want to change the bevel angle

of the cutting edge, adjust the tool rest to the desired angle. With your index finger against the tool rest, roll the blade on the wheel until the entire edge is ground, keeping the bevel flat on the wheel at all times. Continue, checking the blade regularly, until the cutting edge is sharp and the bevel angle is correct. To prevent the blade from overheating, occasionally dip it in water if it is carbon steel, or remove it from the wheel to let it cool if it is high-speed steel. Polish the cutting edge using a felt wheel or a slipstone.

Polishing the Cutting Edge

Move the tool rest out of the way, turn on the grinder, and hold a stick of polishing compound against the felt wheel for a few seconds to impregnate it with abrasive. Then, with the gouge almost vertical, grip the handle in your right hand, hold the blade between the fingers and thumb of your left hand, and set the bevel flat against the

wheel (right). Lightly roll the blade from side to side across the wheel to polish the bevel. A slight burr will form on the inside edge of the tool. To remove it, roll the inside face of the blade against the wheel.

JIG FOR SHARPENING GOUGES

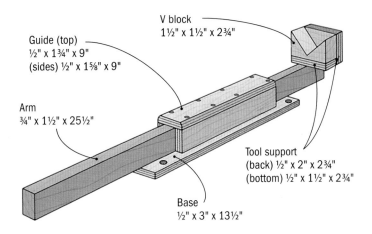

V block
1½" x 1½" x 2¾"

Guide (top)
½" x 1¾" x 9"
(sides) ½" x 1⅝" x 9"

Arm
¾" x 1½" x 25½"

Tool support
(back) ½" x 2" x 2¾"
(bottom) ½" x 1½" x 2¾"

Base
½" x 3" x 13½"

The jig shown above guarantees the tips of longer and larger gouges will contact your grinding wheel at the correct angle to restore the bevel on the cutting edge. The dimensions given in the illustration below will accommodate most turning gouges.

Cut the base and guide from ½-inch plywood. Screw the guide together and fasten it to the base with screws countersunk from underneath. Make sure the opening created by the guide is large enough to allow the arm to slide snugly but freely.

Cut the arm from 1-by-2 stock and the tool support from ¼-inch plywood. Screw the two parts of the tool support together, then fasten the bottom to the arm, flush with one end. For the V block, cut a small wood block to size and saw a 90° wedge out of one side. Glue the block to the support.

To use the jig, secure it to a work surface so the arm lines up directly under the grinding wheel. Seat the gouge handle in the V block and slide the arm so the beveled edge of the gouge lies flat on the grinding wheel. Clamp the arm in place. Then, with the gouge clear of the wheel, switch on the grinder and reposition the tool in the jig. Holding the gouge with both hands, rotate the beveled edge across the wheel (below). Stop occasionally to cool the blade and check the cutting edge periodically until you are satisfied with the results.

Sharpening a Gouge

Set the jig on a work surface so the arm lines up directly under the grinding wheel. Seat the gouge handle in the V block and slide the arm so the beveled edge of the gouge rests flat on the grinding wheel. Clamp the arm in place. Then, with the gouge clear of the wheel, switch on the grinder and reposition the tool in the jig. Holding the gouge with both hands, rotate it from side to side so the beveled edge runs across the wheel (above). Check the cutting edge periodically until the bevel is fully formed.

SPINDLE GOUGE

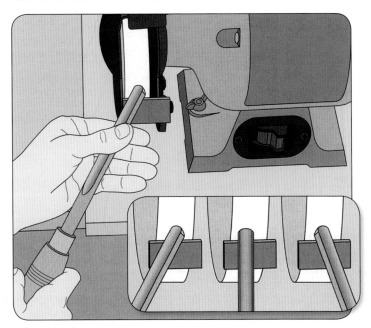

Grinding

Position the guard properly and turn on the grinder. Pinching the blade between the fingers and thumb of one hand, set the blade flat on the tool rest and advance it until the bevel lightly contacts the stone (above). Adjust the tool rest, if desired, to change the bevel angle. If the tool has a square grind, roll the bevel on the stone as you would for a roughing-out gouge (page 61). If the tool has a fingernail-grind, roll the cutting edge on the wheel and pivot the handle from left to right while keeping the bevel flat on the grinding wheel at all times (inset). Continue rolling the blade and moving the tool handle from side to side until the edge is sharpened, stopping occasionally to check the grind and cool the tip.

SPINDLE GOUGE *(continued)*

Honing

Once the bevel has been sharpened on the grinder, use a flat benchstone to polish the tool to a razor-sharp edge. Saturate the stone with oil, then roll the outside bevel across the abrasive surface (top right) to create two microbevels on the cutting edge, as shown on page 70. Use a convex slipstone matching the curvature of the gouge to remove the burr that forms on the inside of the cutting edge. Put a few drops of oil on the slipstone and hone the inside edge until the burr rubs off (bottom right).

Flat benchstone

BOWL GOUGE

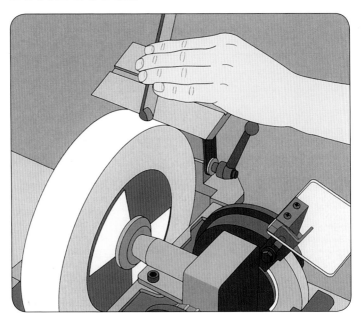

Adjust the tool rest so the bevel will rest flush with the wheel surface, then turn on the grinder. Hold the gouge flat on the tool rest and advance the tool until the bevel is flat on the stone. Then, holding the blade in place, roll the edge across the stone (above), pivoting the handle as necessary to keep the bevel flat on the wheel at all times. Continue until the tool is sharp. The gouge is now ready to use.

SKEW CHISEL

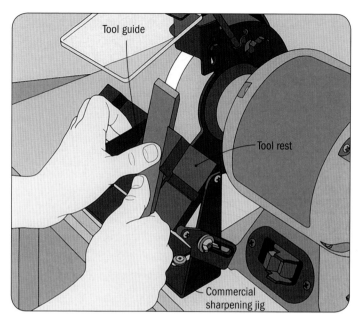

Tool guide

Tool rest

Commercial
sharpening jig

Position a commercial sharpening jig in front of the grinding wheel as close to the wheel as possible without touching it. Set up the jig following the manufacturer's instructions. On the model shown, you can adjust the tool table to the correct angle for any tool—in this case, a straight skew chisel. Place the tool guide supplied with the jig in the groove in the rest and hold the chisel in the guide. Butt one edge of the chisel blade against one side of the groove in the guide so the cutting edge is square to the grinding wheel. Turn on the grinder and advance the tool until the bevel contacts the wheel. Slide the tool guide from side to side to sharpen the bevel. Flip the tool over and repeat the process with the tool against the other edge of the groove in the guide (above). When both bevels are sharpened, hone a microbevel (page 70). The same techniques can be used without benefit of a sharpening jig, using the grinder's tool rest.

RADIUSED SKEW

Using a Jig

Secure the chisel in a commercial jig specially designed for sharpening radiused skew chisels. For the model shown, hold the long edge of the chisel blade against the triangular support piece in the center of the jig and tighten the thumbscrew so the bevel lies flat on the grinding wheel when you sharpen it (above right). Now, position an adjustable tool rest in front of the grinding wheel and set the jig on it, ensuring the pivot pin on the bottom of the jig slides in the hole

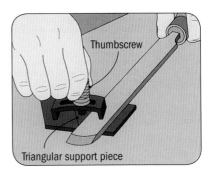

Thumbscrew

Triangular support piece

Adjustable tool rest

in the center of the tool rest. Adjust the angle of the rest so the bevel sits flat on the wheel, then tighten it in position (below right). Turn on the grinder and pivot the bevel across the wheel, keeping the jig pressed down on the tool rest at all times.

RADIUSED SKEW *(continued)*

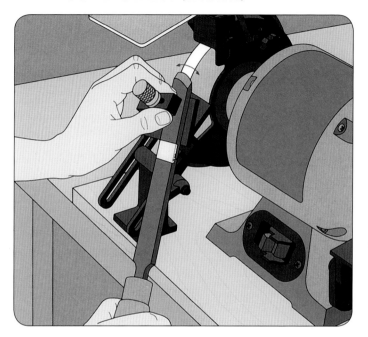

Second Bevel

Once the first bevel is sharpened, turn off the grinder and wrap a piece of masking tape around the chisel blade where it meets the bottom edge of the jig. This will enable you to turn the chisel over and reposition it in the jig so that the second bevel you grind is identical to the first. Remove the chisel from the jig, turn it over, and reposition it so the bottom edge of the jig is aligned with the tape. Turn on the grinder and sharpen the second bevel the same way you ground the first.

MICROBEVELS

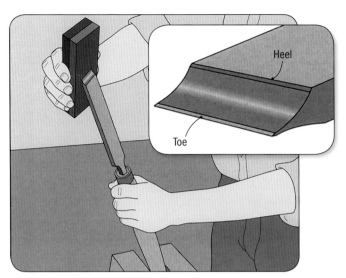

The grinding process creates a rough hollow-ground, or concave, bevel on the tool blade. The heel and toe of the bevel of either straight or radiused blades must be honed to a smooth cutting edge before the chisel is used. To support the chisel, wedge its handle in the lathe bed, then put a few drops of oil on the fine side of a combination stone. Rub the stone across the bevel (above), creating microbevels on both the heel and toe of the bevel (inset). Repeat the procedure on the other side of the tool. As the tool becomes dull with use, you do not need to regrind it. Simply restore the microbevels. After several honings, however, the microbevels will disappear and the bevel will flatten out. At this point, you will have to regrind the tool to restore the hollow-ground bevel.

PARTING TOOL

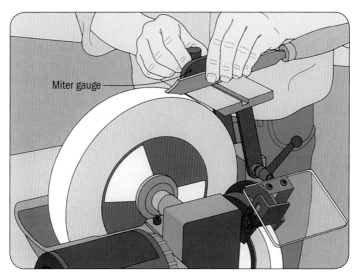

Miter gauge

Adjust the tool rest so the bevel on the parting tool is flat on the wheel. Hold the blade on edge on the tool rest with one side against the miter gauge supplied with the rest, then turn on the grinder and advance the tool until the bevel contacts the wheel. Pressing the tool lightly against the grinder, slide the gauge back and forth until the bevel is sharpened. Repeat the process to sharpen the bevel on the other side (above). Once both bevels are the same and the cutting edge is sharp, hone microbevels as you would on a skew chisel (page 70).

SCRAPER

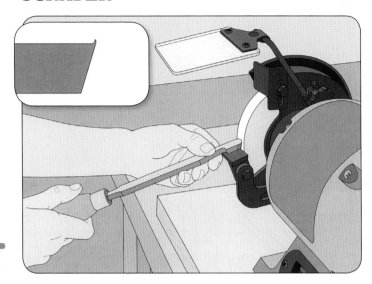

Grinding

Position the guard properly and adjust the tool rest so the bevel on the end of the scraper rests flush against the wheel. Turn on the grinder and hold the blade between the fingers and thumb of one hand. With the blade flat on the tool rest, advance the tool until the bevel lightly contacts the wheel. Pass the entire edge across the wheel (above), moving the handle from side to side. Stop occasionally and run your finger lightly over the end of the tool to feel for a burr (inset). Stop sharpening when a uniform burr forms.

SCRAPER *(continued)*

Burnishing

The secret to raising a burr on a scraper—an essential step in the sharpening process—is to apply light pressure as you hold the blade against the grinding wheel.

Wet grinders do not leave enough of a burr on scraper blades; you can produce a more uniform burr by burnishing the edge. Using firm, even pressure, draw a burnisher across the end of the blade to raise a burr on its top edge.

CHAPTER 6:
Spindle Turning

Of the two main activities practiced on the lathe, spindle turning is the one most closely associated with furniture making.

The process involves mounting a wood blank between the machine's headstock and tailstock and using a variety of turning tools to shape furniture parts, such as chair legs and bedposts, and other decorative pieces. Because the stock is mounted "between centers," the wood grain of the workpiece runs parallel to the axis of the lathe. In bowl, or faceplate turning, which is examined in the next chapter, the grain of a blank is normally perpendicular to the machine's axis of rotation. Despite their differences, both activities do share several things in common: Correct mounting methods, proper tool use, and accurate measurement all are crucial to achieve satisfactory results.

Because spindle turning does not require cutting into end grain, the process involves relatively simple techniques, and no more than three or four tools are required. This makes turning between centers an ideal way to develop a feel for the lathe and good tool technique. On its simplest level, spindle turning is little more than connecting high and low points on a blank with shoulders, beads, and coves.

The chapter that follows introduces spindle turning techniques, from the repertoire of basic spindle cuts (page 76), such as planing, sizing, and taper cuts, to more decorative spindle cuts, such as beads, coves, and balls that will enhance your objects. By sawing the blank in half and regluing it, you can create symmetrical split turnings and other spindle designs (page 98).

As with any activity on the lathe, the best way to learn is by experimentation. Wait until you have mastered the basic techniques before trying to reproduce complex spindle patterns. Use inexpensive wood for your blanks and practice with simple shapes until you are comfortable with the tools.

Turning a well-proportioned leg requires a combination of sound technique and some creativity. In the photo at left, a spindle gouge cuts a bead near the top of the leg. Between the beads and the lathe headstock is the pommel, which is left square so that the leg can be joined to the rail of a table or chair.

SPINDLE CUTS

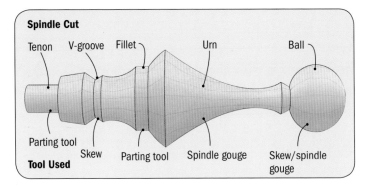

Spindle Cut

Tenon — V-groove — Fillet — Urn — Ball

Parting tool — Skew — Parting tool — Spindle gouge — Skew/spindle gouge

Tool Used

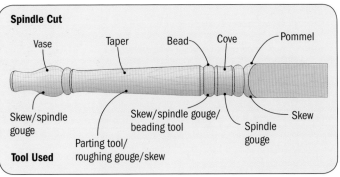

Spindle Cut

Vase — Taper — Bead — Cove — Pommel

Skew/spindle gouge — Skew/spindle gouge/ beading tool — Spindle gouge — Skew

Parting tool/ roughing gouge/skew

Tool Used

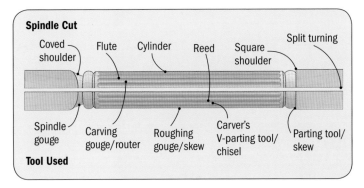

Spindle Cut

Coved shoulder — Flute — Cylinder — Reed — Square shoulder — Split turning

Spindle gouge — Carving gouge/router — Roughing gouge/skew — Carver's V-parting tool/ chisel — Parting tool/ skew

Tool Used

SPINDLE CUTS *(continued)*

Producing a tool handle on the lathe is an ideal project for the novice wood turner. In the photo above, a Jacobs chuck in the tailstock holds a drill bit as it bores a hole for the tang at the handle-end of the blade.

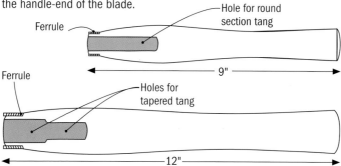

Hole for round section tang

Ferrule

← 9" →

Ferrule

Holes for tapered tang

← 12" →

SETTING UP

All spindle work starts with a square blank. The more perfect the square, the better. By starting with blanks that are straight, free of defects, squared on the jointer, and properly centered on the lathe, you can avoid catching a tool on the workpiece or splitting the wood.

Two keys to smooth spindle work are using proper tool control (page 81) and cutting in the direction of the wood grain (page 83). Stance and body movement are just as important as how you hold a tool. A good working stance is to stand with your feet apart and comfortably balanced. Your body should move smoothly with the tool. Never stand so far away from the lathe that you are forced to lean forward. With thicker workpieces, your hip or elbow can provide support for the tool.

While spindle turning is relatively safe, remember not to become too casual in your approach. Improperly used, the lathe causes injuries like any other woodworking machine.

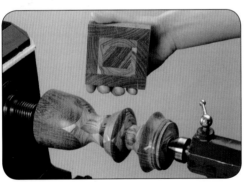

Laminated or "sandwich" blanks can yield interesting geometric patterns when they are turned between centers. The blank for the vase shown in the photo above was made by gluing layers of tulipwood and purpleheart around a square zebrawood core. A range of different patterns can be produced by alternating the manner in which the layers are glued up.

SETTING UP *(continued)*

Marking Centers

To mount a blank on the lathe for spindle turning, find each end's center. Make sure the blank is square, and then hold it on end and mark two lines across one end from corner to corner (right). Repeat at other end. The lines intersect at the centers. Next, use a four-spur drive center and a mallet to make indentations at the centers. Align the centerpoint of the drive center over the centers and strike sharply with the mallet (inset); make sure the spurs bite into the wood. Repeat at other end. Insert the drive center in the lathe's headstock. Do not strike the drive center while it is mounted in the headstocks that could damage the lathe's bearings.

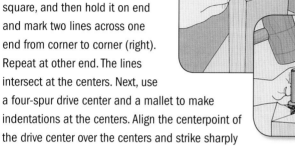

Four spur drive center

Mounting the Blank

To mount the blank between centers, start by butting one end against the tailstock's live center. Supporting the blank's other end with one hand, slide the tailstock toward the headstock until the spurs of the drive center engage the indentations you made in "Marking Centers" (right). Secure the tailstock with the locking lever, then advance the tailstock spindle and live center by turning the handwheel until the blank is held firmly between the centers. Secure the tailstock spindle with the spindle lock.

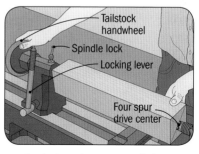

Tailstock handwheel
Spindle lock
Locking lever
Four spur drive center

SETTING UP *(continued)*

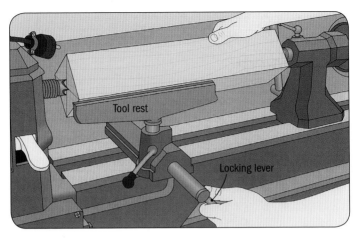

Tool rest

Locking lever

Tool Rest

Align the tool rest parallel to the blank, positioning it close to the workpiece without making contact when the blank spins. With the lathe switched off, rotate the blank by hand to ensure it does not hit the tool rest (above). The gap between the tool rest and the blank should be the same at both ends; adjust the rest, if necessary. Although experienced turners adjust the height of the tool rest according to personal preference, a good place to start is with the tool rest at or slightly below the center of the blank. This way, your tools will cut above the center of the blank. Tighten the tool rest in position with the locking lever.

TOOL CONTROL

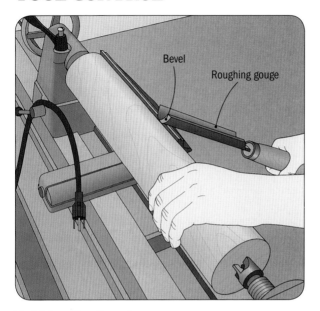

Bevel

Roughing gouge

Rubbing the Bevel

The first rule of tool control in turning is to ensure the blade's bevel rubs against the stock as the cutting edge slices into the wood. The principle is key to producing smooth, clean cuts with tools such as the spindle gouge and the skew chisel. To master the basic technique, unplug the lathe and mount a cylindrical blank between centers. Brace a tool—in this case a roughing gouge—on the tool rest so its bevel rests on the stock. Gripping the tool with one hand, tilt the handle down. Use your free hand to rotate the blank in a clockwise direction; the bevel should rub smoothly against the work (above).

TOOL CONTROL *(continued)*

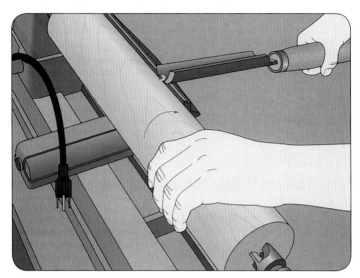

Starting the Cut

Once the bevel is rubbing, slowly raise the tool handle; the cutting edge should begin to slice the wood (above). Control the depth of cut by the height of the handle; the higher it is raised, the more wood is removed. Do not go so far that the bevel stops rubbing against the wood, or the tool will catch on the spinning blank.

TOOL CONTROL *(continued)*

Making the Cut

Slowly angle the tool in the direction of cut and slide it along the workpiece (right), aligning your upper body behind the tool throughout the cut. As you move, rotate the tool slightly in the direction of cut to avoid catching the blade. Now, plug in the lathe, turn it on, and repeat Steps 1 through 3 with the blank spinning. When you produce fine shavings and leave a smooth surface requiring little sanding, the tool is cutting properly.

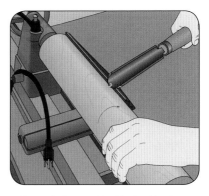

Cutting Downhill

Bundles of fibers aligned in one direction, called the grain direction, compose wood. Just as pushing a hand plane against the grain causes tearout, working against the grain with a turning tool produces rough cuts and leads to kickback. As shown by the arrows in the illustration above, the smoothest spindle turning cuts are made in a downhill direction—from a high point to a low point on the workpiece. Such cuts are either with, across, or at an angle to the grain. Never cut uphill, or the tool digs into the wood causing splintering and shearing of wood fibers, and leaving a rough surface on the blank.

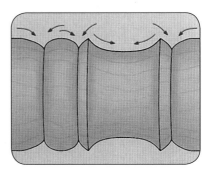

BASIC CUTS

The basic spindle cuts shown in this section will help sharpen your turning abilities for more challenging projects you tackle later on. The cuts include roughing, planing, peeling, V-cuts, shoulder cuts, and parting off.

Four tools are used for most basic spindle cuts: the roughing gouge, the spindle gouge, the skew chisel, and the parting tool. They are typically held in one of two grips: overhand or underhand. The overhand grip is commonly used to guide a tool along the tool rest, such as when roughing down a blank (page 85). The underhand grip is used for finer control (below).

One bonus of spindle turning is you can see the results of your cuts as you go. As you gain experience, you will also become familiar with the various sounds of the turning process. From your first roughing cuts to a final planing cut, there is a definite sequence of sounds produced as wood is turned. By listening closely to the succession of sounds emitted by the lathe, you will be able to use your ears—as well as your eyes—to assess the progress of your work.

Because it is spinning at high speeds, a blank mounted between centers provides the turner with an immediate and continual visual check of a project's progress. At left, a roughing gouge brings a small baseball bat to its final shape.

TURNING A CYLINDER

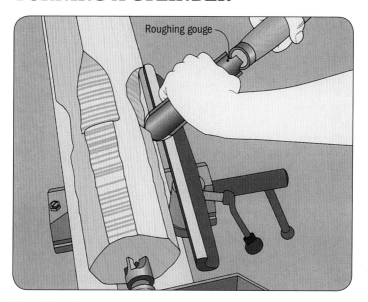

Roughing gouge

Roughing Down

Mount your blank between centers and set the appropriate speed for the size of the workpiece. Holding a roughing gouge with an overhand grip, brace the blade on the tool rest. Cut very lightly into the blank, making sure the bevel rubs against the stock. Move the gouge smoothly along the tool rest. (If your blank is longer than the tool rest, rough out the cylinder in two or more steps.) The gouge begins rounding the corners of the workpiece. Continue making successively deeper passes along the blank, raising the handle of the tool slightly with each pass, until the edges are completely rounded and you have a cylinder. Adjust the position of the tool rest as you progress to keep it close to the blank.

TURNING A CYLINDER *(continued)*

Finishing Cuts

Once one section of the blank is cylindrical, reposition the tool rest and round over the rest of the workpiece (right). To check the smoothness of the blank, set the bottom of the gouge blade on the spinning blank (below). The blade should ride smoothly on the surface. If it bounces, the surface is not yet perfectly round.

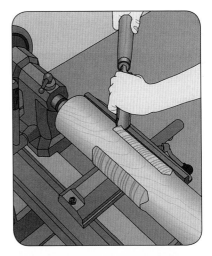

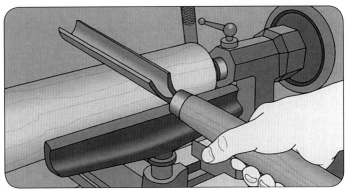

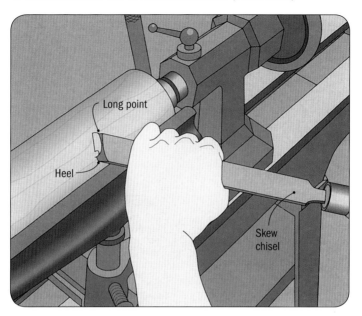

Planing Smooth

Use a skew chisel to plane the cylinder to a smooth finish. Holding the tool with an overhand grip, set the blade on the rest so its long point is above the blank and its bevel is inclined in the direction of the cut; this is typically about 65° to the axis of the wood. Switch on the lathe and raise the handle slightly, bringing the cutting edge of the chisel into contact with the wood. Move the blade along the tool rest (above), letting its bevel rub; do not let its heel or long point dig into the wood. The center of the cutting edge should produce a series of thin shavings.

TURNING A CYLINDER *(continued)*

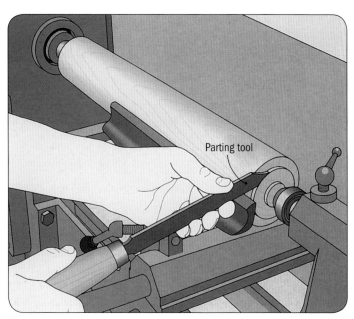

Parting tool

Trim to Length

Once you have planed the cylinder smooth, use a parting tool to cut it to
length. Mark a cutting line on the spinning cylinder with a pencil. Then,
holding a parting tool edge-up on the tool rest as shown (above), raise
the handle slightly so the blade cuts into the blank. Clean up the end
grain with a skew chisel. If you have further shaping to do on the blank,
cut about two-thirds of the way through the cylinder so it remains on
the lathe. If all you wish to make is a cylinder, continue the cut to near
the center of the blank, then turn off the lathe and cut away the cylinder
with a handsaw.

TURNING A CYLINDER *(continued)*

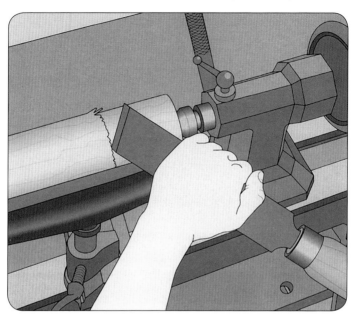

Peeling Cuts

Peeling is an alternate way of quickly smoothing a cylinder; use a large skew chisel instead of a roughing gouge. A peeling cut is similar to a planing cut (page 87), except you intentionally dig the heel of the chisel into the blank with the bevel rubbing on the stock (above). The heel will lift a circle of shavings as you guide the chisel along the tool rest. Because it removes a lot of stock and requires more control than a planing cut, peeling is more difficult to master, and should be done carefully.

MAKING TAPERS

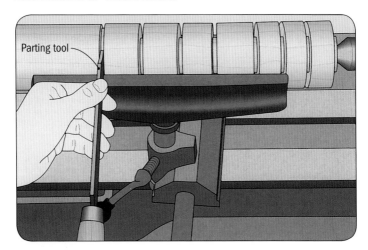

Parting tool

Sizing Cuts

If you are not copying a particular piece, make a hardboard template of the taper. (The template, illustrated on page 91, indicates the finished diameter of the blank at several different points along its length.) Turn your blank into a cylinder, then make a series of sizing cuts with a parting tool from one end of the blank to the other. Holding the parting tool with an underhand grip edge-up on the tool rest, raise the handle slightly so the blade cuts into the cylinder. Continue to raise the handle until the cut reaches the required depth (above). Each cut should penetrate to the finished diameter of the workpiece at that point; check your progress with calipers (page 91). Twist the tool slightly from side to side as you make the cut in order to minimize friction and to prevent the blade from jamming.

MAKING TAPERS *(continued)*

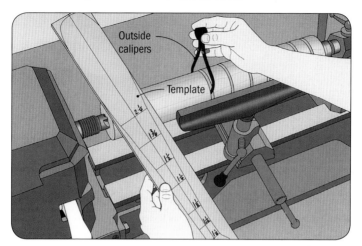

Checking Depth

Adjust a pair of outside calipers to one of the dimensions of the taper as marked on your template. Then check the diameter of the blank at the corresponding sizing cut (above). Deepen the cut if necessary until the measurements on the template and the diameter of the cut are equal. Repeat for the remaining sizing cuts.

MAKING TAPERS *(continued)*

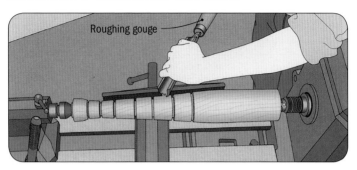

Roughing gouge

Roughing the Taper

After finishing all of the sizing cuts, use a roughing gouge to clear out the waste between cuts. Follow the same procedure you would use to rough out a cylinder (page 85), holding the tool with an overhand grip and always working in a downhill direction to avoid tearout (above). Joining the sizing cuts will create a taper along the length of the workpiece. Then use a skew chisel to plane the taper smooth. Work in a downhill direction.

Preset Calipers

If you are spindle turning several identical pieces on the lathe, you can speed up the process by adjusting separate calipers for each feature of the blanks (right). For the leg shown here, one pair is adjusted for the thicker part of the leg, another is set for the bead below it, and a third is adjusted for the narrow section near the bottom of the leg. This will save you the trouble of continually readjusting a single pair of calipers. To avoid confusing the settings, attach a numbered strip of tape to each instrument.

MAKING GROOVES

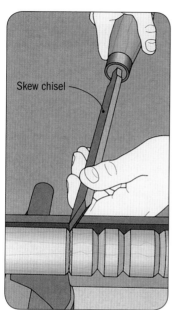

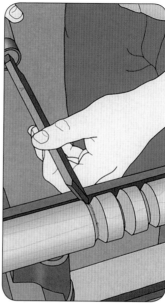

Skew chisel

Turn a cylinder (page 85), then mark the location of the grooves with a pencil. Make the cuts with a skew chisel. At each location mark, start with the long point of the chisel pointing forward and raise the handle, allowing the point of the blade to cut to the required depth. Then make a cut on each side of the initial cut, arcing the chisel to the side so a portion of the bevel rubs against the edge of the groove (above left). To widen the groove, repeat the side cuts (above right).

COVED SHOULDERS

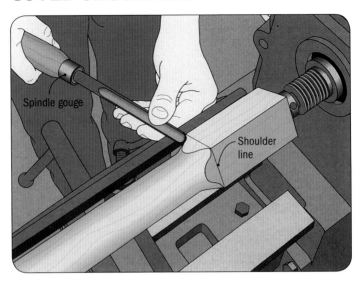

Spindle gouge

Shoulder line

Coved Shoulders

Coved shoulders are a common feature of chair legs. To make the cut, start by scribing a shoulder line around the four sides of the blank to separate its round and square sections. Turn the round section of the blank to a cylinder (page 85), tapering the leg if desired (page 90). Next, use a spindle gouge to turn the coved shoulder. Holding the tool with an underhand grip at an angle to the blank, align its bevel with the direction of cut and its flute with the shoulder line. Raise the handle and pivot the tool on the tool rest, making a slicing cut "downhill" toward the tailstock end. Define the cove with a series of successively deeper cuts.

SQUARE SHOULDERS

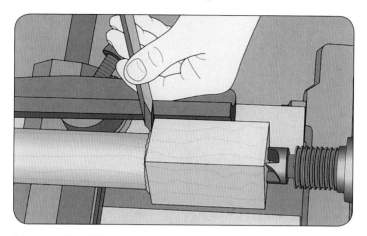

Making the Shoulder

Mark a shoulder line on the blank and turn the round section into a cylinder (page 85), leaving the square section intact. Then use a skew chisel to clean up the transition between the square and round segments of the workpiece. Start by holding the tool edge up so that its long point and part of the bevel are aligned with the shoulder line. Slowly raise the handle, making a clean slicing cut down to the round portion of the workpiece (above).

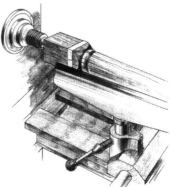

If you are turning pieces requiring a sharp division between turned and square sections, such as the pommel at the top of a chair leg, wrap duct or masking tape around the blank at the transition line before turning (right). The tape provides a clear stopping mark.

SQUARE SHOULDERS *(continued)*

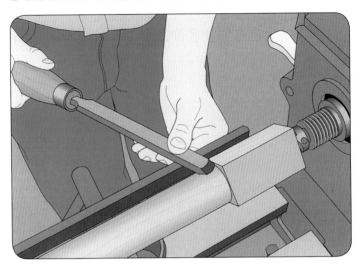

Cleaning Up

Set the chisel's bevel flat on the round section and carefully touch the heel of the cutting edge against the shoulder to cut away any remaining waste (above).

POMMELS

Vee Cut

Mark a shoulder line around the four sides of a blank to separate the pommel from the cylindrical section of the leg. (For this procedure, the blank is turned into a cylinder after the pommel is cut.) Turn a V-groove in the workpiece with a skew chisel (page 93),

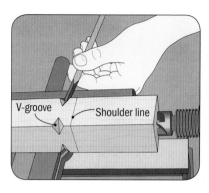

V-groove
Shoulder line

starting about ½ inch away from the shoulder line (above). Deepen the groove until it runs completely around the workpiece.

Shaping the Pommel

After finishing the V-groove, turn the pommel as you would to widen the groove, cutting with the long point of the chisel pointed forward. Arc the chisel from side to side so the bevel rubs against the edges of the groove walls as you cut

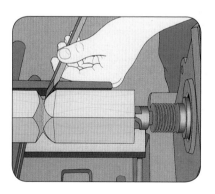

them (right). Turn off the lathe after each cut to check the shape of the pommel; stop when you reach the shoulder line. Finally, turn the round portion of the workpiece into a cylinder (page 85).

Pommels

PARTING OFF

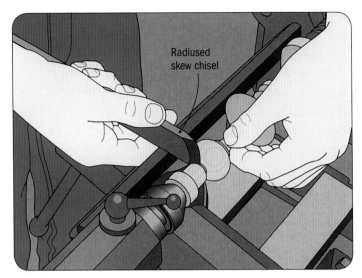

Radiused
skew chisel

Once you have finished turning a spindle project, it may be necessary
to separate it from the waste wood used to hold the workpiece between
centers. For turnings with square ends, make a sizing cut (page 90) right
through the workpiece with a parting tool. For turnings with rounded
ends, like the urn finial shown above, use a skew chisel or radiused skew
chisel to preserve the curved shape. Holding the tool with an underhand
grip, make a slicing cut with the long point of the blade as you would
round a pommel (page 97). Support the turning with your hand, keeping
your fingers well clear of the tool rest and being careful not to grip the
spinning workpiece. Make a series of deeper V-cuts until the finished
turning breaks loose from the waste. Remove the workpiece from the
lathe and saw off the waste at the other end.

TENONS

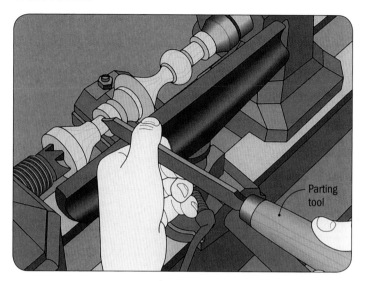

Parting
tool

If you intend to join your workpiece to another part of the finished work with a round mortise-and-tenon joint, turn a tenon at the end of the blank before parting it off. Holding a parting tool with an underhand grip, turn the tenon in the waste section of the blank (above). Make a series of sizing cuts, checking the tenon's diameter with calipers as you go.

THIN TURNINGS

It is difficult to turn long, thin blanks between centers without gouging the surface because the turning often flexes and vibrates on the lathe, resulting in chatter. You can eliminate this problem by using a commercial steady rest, which supports thin spindle work between centers. The model shown in the photo above slides along the lathe bed and adjusts for turnings up to 2¼ inches in diameter.

HAND SUPPORT

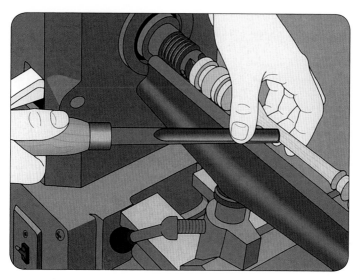

When shaping thin spindle work, it is important to support the workpiece and reduce vibration. If you do not have a steady rest, you can use one of your hands. As you turn the blank, cradle it in the fingers of your left hand while bracing the tool against the rest with the thumb (above). Keep your fingers clear of the tool blade and avoid applying excessive pressure on the turning.

CHAPTER 7:
Finishing Spindles

There is a widespread belief among wood turners that if a turning needs to be sanded, then the tools used to produce it were either dull or used improperly. There is more than a little truth behind this opinion; a smooth and clean turning needs no sanding. A surface cut cleanly by tools is superior to a sanded surface; sanding is performed against the grain and a finish will only magnify the blemishes. Until you develop into a proficient enough turner to skip sandpaper altogether, use it sparingly, only to smooth the wood, never to actually shape it. Start with 100 grit and work up to 280 grit.

A spindle turning is best finished right on the lathe. A good finish seals the wood from dust and moisture while bringing out the natural beauty of the wood. Because they tend to obscure rather than enhance grain, stains are rarely used. Turnings are often finished with a combination oil-and-wax finish, although higher-gloss finishes, such as lacquer, can be applied; see the chart on page 103 for a selection of appropriate products. As with sanding on the lathe, run the machine at a slow speed to avoid splashing, always keep the tool rest clear of the work, and finish the turning from underneath. Avoid using large cloths, as they can get snagged and pull your fingers into the spinning work.

CHOOSING A FINISH

TYPE OF FINISH	FINISHING PRODUCTS	CHARACTERISTICS AND USES	METHODS OF APPLICATION
Penetrating oils	Tung oil, Danish oil	Natural finish that penetrates the wood and hardens to a thin, moisture-resistant film as it dries. Used for general spindle turnings, penetrating oils build up a transparent matte to semigloss finish with repeated applications.	Applied with cotton cloth.
Non-toxic penetrating oils	Pure walnut oil, salad oil, mineral oil	These are natural oils. Pure walnut oil and salad oil are used on kitchen implements and salad bowls, mineral oil is used on turned toys such as children's rattles.	Applied with cotton cloth.
High-gloss finishes	Lacquer, shellac	Solvent-release finishes that dry quickly to a clear, hard finish; a glossy finish can be built up with repeated applications. Used on vases, bowls, platters and specialty turnings where a high gloss is desired.	Lacquer is brushed or sprayed on turning while lathe is off, then buffed and burnished with cotton cloth and fine abrasives while work is spinning; shellac is applied with cotton cloth and fine abrasives.
Waxes	Carnauba, beeswax, paste wax	Used on general spindle turnings to seal and protect oiled workpieces while imparting a high polish. Carnauba is a hard, brittle vegetable wax; commercial paste wax is a blend of carnauba and softer beeswax.	Applied with cotton cloth; carnauba can be applied by stick.

SANDING SPINDLES

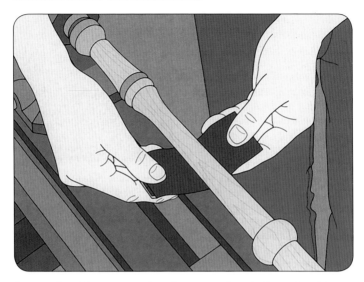

Remove the tool rest. To sand the flat areas of a spindle turning, fold a piece of sandpaper in thirds to prevent the paper from slipping. Switch on the lathe and, holding the paper in both hands, lift the paper to the turning from underneath. Work with the grain along the length of the work as much as possible. Stop sanding periodically to prevent burning. Once the scratches from the previous grit have been smoothed away, move to a finer paper.

SANDING COVES AND BEADS

Sand coves by bending the sandpaper into a U shape so it contacts the concave surface. Holding the paper in both hands, smooth the cove from directly above (top). Narrow coves can be sanded by wrapping the paper around a dowel of the appropriate diameter. Sand beads or pommels holding the paper vertically and rolling from side to side to contact the wood (bottom). Be careful that your fingers are not struck by the square pommel corners.

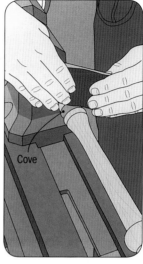

Cove

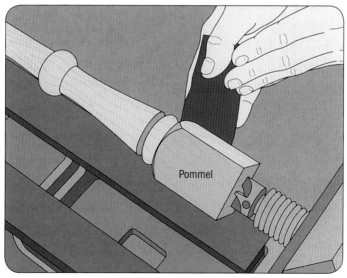

Pommel

APPLYING OIL

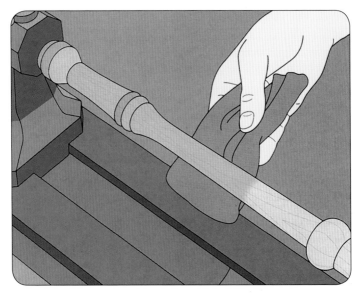

Set the lathe to a slow speed to prevent the oil from splashing. Apply some oil to a soft cotton cloth and rub it into the spinning wood from underneath (above); make sure the cloth is not wrapped around your fingers. Let the turning dry, and repeat as many times as needed until the oil penetrates the wood. If desired, you can sand the turning with 320-grit sandpaper and rub out the finish with fine abrasives such as pumice or rottenstone and a rag. Finally, rub the turning with wood shavings (photo, page 103) to give it a final burnishing.

APPLYING WAX

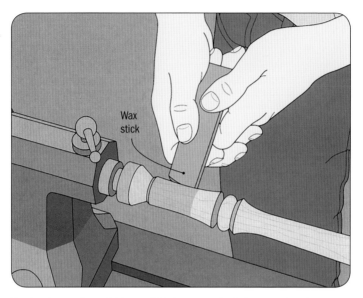

Wax stick

To give the turning a higher polish, increase the lathe speed and apply a wax finish. If you are using a soft wax, apply it with a soft cloth as you would oil. If you are using a turner's wax stick, hold the stick gently against the spinning workpiece (above), and apply a thin layer to the surface. Move the wax stick quickly along the turning to prevent too much buildup. With either wax, buff the turning with a clean cotton cloth; keep rubbing until the wax is melted and the desired gloss is achieved.

CHAPTER 8:

Faceplate Turning

There is something uniquely rewarding about faceplate turning—transforming a piece of rough lumber into a smooth, symmetrical bowl. From start to finish, the entire process takes place on a lathe. There is no assembly, joinery, or fabrication of other parts. The product is complete in this single process.

Faceplate turning also offers the wood turner a great deal of design freedom. True, there are certain practical considerations. What will the bowl hold? How strong does it need to be? But there is also much room for experimentation and improvisation in distinguishing factors ranging from the shape of the bowl and its base to the thickness of its walls.

The options increase with a turner's skill. For beginners, it is best first to master some traditional shapes and profiles. This chapter shows how to produce two relatively easy bowl designs. Completing these projects helps you develop the skills needed to give free reign to your creativity.

Most bowl-turning projects follow the same basic sequence. Begin by mounting what will be the top of the bowl to the lathe, then shape the outside, sand and finish the surface, and prepare the base for mounting. Then reverse the bowl and true and shape the rim. Finally, turn the inside of the bowl, sand and finish it, and reverse the bowl one last time to complete the base and remove evidence of your mounting method.

Before you begin turning, you will need to find a suitable way to mount your blank on the lathe. Traditionally, this is done by screwing or taping the stock to a faceplate or gluing it to a block attached to the faceplate. More recently, turners have used a variety of chucks to clamp their work. Chucks can hold small and oddly shaped pieces, and are excellent for gripping the rim of a bowl to turn the base. Chucks also save time if you are turning a series of similar pieces. No matter what you use to hold a blank, you are sure to find faceplate turning a rewarding and challenging experience.

A gouge shapes the base of a bowl. The recess at the center of the base will be used to rechuck the bowl to the lathe so the inside can be hollowed out.

SELECTING WOOD FOR BOWLS

While you can turn a bowl from dry, seasoned wood, it is much more difficult than working with green, unseasoned wood. The trade-off is, green or unseasoned wood moves and distorts as it dries. Some turners turn the green blank extra-thick, then let the wood dry before completing the bowl. Others turn the final shape in the first place, and enjoy the distortion that occurs as the wood naturally dries.

Whether you are turning fresh-cut wood from a log, or a seasoned blank of wood, the way you orient the wood on the lathe has a lot to do with the figure you will see in the finished bowl. These diagrams show the basic possibilities.

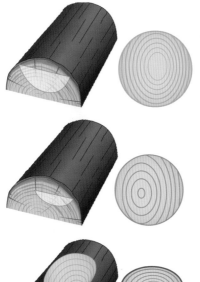

Turning the bowl so the pith of the log is at the bottom means the annual rings will form circles or ovals on the inside.

Shifting the blank away from the center of the log will also shift the pattern made by the annual rings.

Many turners enjoy including the bark-covered outside of the log in the bowl form. Oriented this way, the bark will make a continuous band around the edge of the bowl–provided the turner has enough skill to avoid disturbing it as he works.

SELECTING WOOD FOR BOWLS *(continued)*

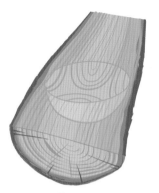

The simplest way to turn a bowl is with its outside shape echoing the curve of the annual rings in the wood. This orientation is possible whether the wood is green or seasoned.

The inside of the bowl will display a hyperbolic pattern.

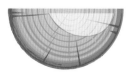

Cutting the blank off the center of the log will shift the pattern of the wood figure.

MOUNTING METHODS

The methods of mounting a blank for faceplate turning far outnumber the techniques used to produce the pieces themselves. The traditional work-holding device, the faceplate (right), is still popular for securing the top of a bowl to turn the bottom; screws are driven into wood that will be hollowed out later to form the mouth of the vessel. Rather than driving screws into your blank, you can use a faceplate for mounting with a glue block (page 114), a paper joint (page 115), or double-sided tape (page 116). Once the turning is finished, the workpiece is pried, sawn, or parted off the auxiliary block—or, in the case of double-sided tape, the faceplate. In general, yellow glue should be used with glue blocks except when you are turning green wood, for which gap-filling cyanoacrylate adhesive is the best choice.

The alternative to a faceplate is a chuck, and the number of commercial models available to wood turners has increased in recent years. Most standard chucking methods are shown in the following pages. The scroll chuck (page 120), which uses three or four contracting or expanding jaws to clamp stock, is a prime example. It is quick and easy to use and the jaws leave no visible marks on the workpiece. In addition, some models can be fitted with rubber posts for holding the rim of a nearly finished bowl so the bottom can be turned (page 121). However, the spinning jaws represent a two-fold danger. First, if you get too close, they can inflict a serious wound. Second, and most important, if you over-expand the jaws, they can come loose and fly away from the tool, causing injury.

If you use a chuck, read the owner's manual carefully and follow all the safety precautions, particularly those regarding the size of the workpiece and the chuck capacity. Commercial chucks can also be expensive. The shop-made example shown on page 122 is handy and costs almost nothing to build. Other traditional wooden chuck designs can be made just as easily and tailored for your work.

MOUNTING METHODS *(continued)*

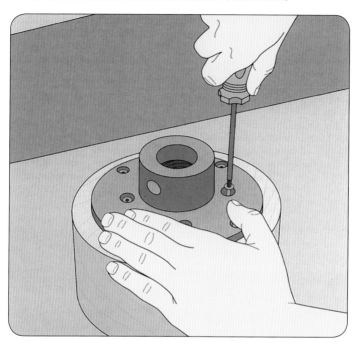

Faceplate

A faceplate provides a reliable and safe method of mounting stock to the headstock, but you must be careful not to drive screws into any wood that will remain in the finished bowl. Rough-cut your blank to a circle on the band saw, then set it on a work surface. Center the faceplate on top of the bowl blank and fasten it in place (above). Then, mount the faceplate to the headstock spindle of the lathe.

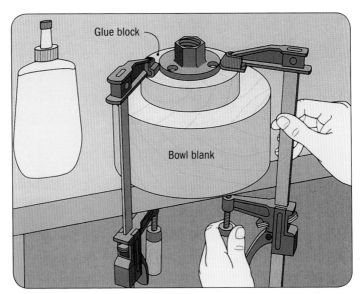

Glue Block

The glue block mounting method relies on adhesives that provide a solid hold without penetrating too deeply into the wood. Usually, yellow glue will do the job. Make sure the bottom of the bowl blank is even enough to form a clean joint with the glue block; smooth the surface with a hand plane, if necessary. To fashion the glue block, cut a wood block into a circle slightly larger than the diameter of your faceplate. The block should be thick enough to hold the screws that will attach it to the faceplate. Fasten the block to the faceplate, then spread an even coating of yellow glue on the block and center it on the bowl blank. Use two clamps to secure the pieces together with even pressure and allow the adhesive to cure (above). Once the turning is done, the glue block can be parted off from the blank.

MOUNTING METHODS *(continued)*

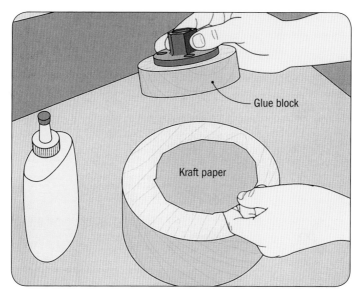

Glue block

Kraft paper

Paper Joint

The paper joint is identical to the glue block method described above, except that a sheet of kraft paper is sandwiched between the glue block and the bowl blank. The paper allows the pieces to be pried apart once the bowl is turned. Screw the faceplate to the glue block, ensuring the screws do not pass through the block. Then spread a thin layer of glue on the bottom of the bowl blank and on the glue block. Place a piece of kraft paper slightly larger than the glue block on the workpiece, set the glue block on the paper (above), then clamp the assembly as you would a glue joint.

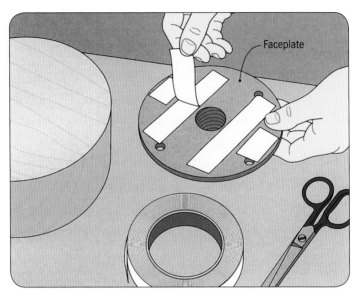

Faceplate

Double-stick Tape

Double-sided turning tape provides a simple way to secure a lightweight blank for faceplate turning. Cut strips of two-sided turning tape to cover as much of the faceplate as possible. Remove the backing paper from one side of the strips and fix them on the faceplate. Then, peel the paper off the other side of the tape (above). Press the faceplate on the blank, centering it as well as possible on the stock.

MOUNTING METHODS *(continued)*

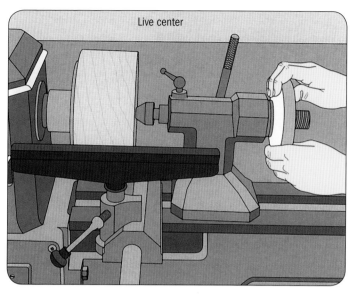

Live center

Tailstock Pressure

Use pressure from the tailstock to reinforce the tape bond between the faceplate and the turning blank. Install the faceplate on the headstock spindle. Then insert a live center in the tailstock and slide it against the blank. Turn the hand-wheel to increase the pressure (above). You can now either move the tailstock away from the blank and shape the outside of the bowl or leave the tailstock in place. Do not leave the blank on the lathe for an extended time, because gravity loosens the holding power of the tape; instead, when you stop work, remove the faceplate from the headstock and set the assembly down flat.

CENTERING JIGS

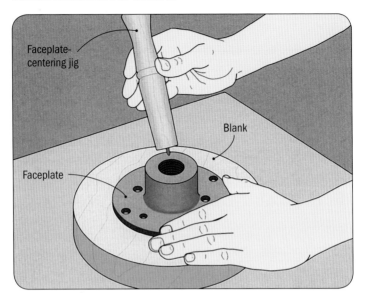

Faceplate-centering jig

Blank

Faceplate

To center your lathe's faceplate on a circular blank, use the jig shown above. Turn a piece of wood into a cylinder the same diameter as the faceplate's threaded hole, tapering the end slightly. (You may wish to form a handle at the top of the jig.) Drive a nail into the center of the tapered end, cut off the nail head, and grind a sharp point. To use the jig, mark the center of the blank with an awl and set the faceplate on the workpiece with the mark in the middle of the threaded hole. Insert the jig in the hole (above), and "feel" for the mark with the nail tip. Holding the jig in place, screw the faceplate to the blank.

CENTERING JIGS (continued)

Acrylic plastic disk

Skew chisel

The jig shown above will enable you to center a faceplate on an irregularly shaped blank. Cut pieces of ¼-inch clear acrylic plastic and ¾-inch plywood into 12-inch-diameter disks. Leaving the paper backing on both sides of the plastic, attach the two together with double-sided tape and a

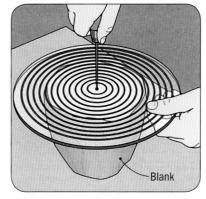

Blank

central screw. Mount them to your faceplate so the plastic is facing out. Use a skew chisel to cut a series of equally spaced, concentric rings in the disk (top). Remove the plastic from the plywood and spray it with black paint. Once the paint has dried, peel the backing paper off both sides of the plastic. To use the jig, position the blank so as much of it as possible is within one of the rings and mark the center with an awl (bottom).

SCROLL CHUCK (CONTRACTING)

Attaching the Chuck

Attach scroll chucks to the base of a bowl blank after the outside of the blank has been shaped (page 134). For a chuck with contracting jaws, turn a dovetailed tenon on the bottom of the blank. (Follow the manufacturer's

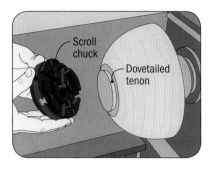

instructions for the appropriate size of the tenon.) Adjust the jaws of the chuck so they will slip over the tenon (above). Hand-tighten the jaws around the tenon by turning the scroll ring, then remove the blank from the lathe and unscrew the faceplate.

Tightening the Jaws

Thread the chuck onto the headstock of your lathe, then finish tightening the chuck jaws around the tenon following the manufacturer's instructions. For the model shown, tighten the chuck scroll ring while holding the chuck body stationary. If your lathe has a spindle lock, hold the spindle steady with it

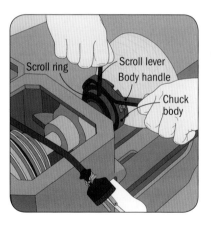

and use the scroll lever to tighten the scroll ring. If your machine has no spindle lock, use the body handle to hold the chuck body as you tighten the scroll ring (right).

SCROLL CHUCK (EXPANDING)

Fitting the Chuck in the Recess

To attach a scroll chuck with expanding jaws to a bowl blank, first turn a dovetailed recess in the bottom of the bowl to suit the jaws (page 120). (Follow the manufacturer's instructions

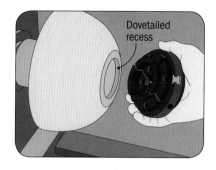

Dovetailed recess

for the size of the recess.) Then fit the jaws into the recess and turn the scroll ring by hand to secure the chuck. Remove the blank from the lathe and unscrew the faceplate.

Tightening the Chuck

Set the blank face down on a work surface and tighten the jaws in the recess following the manufacturer's instructions. For the model shown, insert the scroll lever in the scroll ring and the body handle in the chuck body (below), and tighten the ring and body against each other until the jaws grip the walls of the recess tightly.

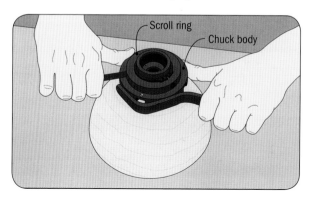

Scroll ring

Chuck body

CONTRACTION CHUCK

The contraction chuck shown at right can be fashioned from a small block of wood. The dimensions in the illustration enable the jig to secure the bottom of a large-sized goblet blank to the lathe headstock.

Dovetailed rim

Hose clamp

Contraction chuck
Length: 3¾"
Diameter: 3¾"

Faceplate

To make the jig, mount a blank on the headstock and turn it to a cylinder. Use a round-nose scraper to hollow out a recess about 1¼ inch deep in the center of the cylinder (below, left). Follow the same procedure as you would to hollow out a goblet, leaving the walls of the chuck about ¼ inch thick. Use a side-cutting scraper to remove additional wood just below the top edge of the rim, creating a dovetailed lip around the inside edge. This will mesh with a dovetailed tenon you will turn in the bottom of your workpiece, helping to hold it in the chuck. Make sure you brace each scraper on the tool rest as you make these cuts.

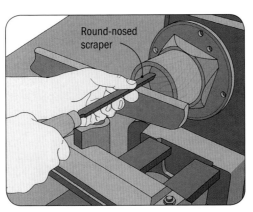

Round-nosed scraper

Handscrew

CONTRACTION CHUCK *(continued)*

Bore four ⅜ inch holes around the circumference, spaced 90° apart and located 1¼ inch below the rim of the chuck, flush with the bottom of the recess. For the first hole, clamp the drive shaft with a handscrew to prevent the spindle from rotating. To drill the remaining holes, remove the hand-screw, rotate the chuck 90°, and clamp the drive shaft again (facing page, bottom right). Remove the faceplate from the headstock and secure it in a vise. Use a handsaw to cut four kerfs from the rim into the holes

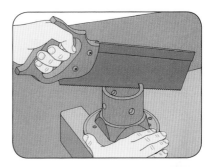

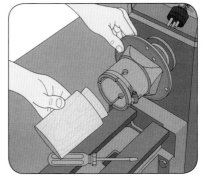

you drilled (top). The cuts define the jaws of your chuck. Widen the kerfs to ⅛ inch using a chisel, then install a hose clamp around the chuck.

To use the chuck, turn a dovetailed tenon on your workpiece slightly smaller than the diameter of the recess in the jig, mount the chuck and faceplate on the lathe headstock, and insert the workpiece in the chuck (bottom). Tighten the hose clamp to secure the stock in place.

Contraction Chuck

SCREW CHUCK

Preparing the Blank

The screw chuck is easy to use, but it is not strong enough to hold large blanks or secure end grain. Refer to the manufacturer's instructions for limitations on the size of blanks you can use. For the model shown below, a maximum

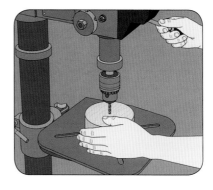

diameter-to-length ratio of 3:1 is recommended. Additional support can be provided for large blanks by sliding the tailstock against the work as you turn the bowl. To prepare your blank for the screw chuck, plane the contacting face of the blank so the chuck's collar will fit flush against it. Bore a pilot hole into the center of the blank to accommodate the chuck screw (above)—in this case, a ¼-inch hole to a depth of 1 inch.

Mounting

Screw the chuck to the headstock spindle of the lathe, then attach the blank to the chuck (below). Screw on the blank until it sits firmly against the screw collar.

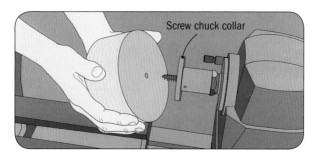

Screw chuck collar

SPLIT-RING CHUCK

The three-way split ring chuck is ideal for securing small goblet blanks and other pieces with grain running the length of the piece. Prepare your blank following the manufacturer's instructions. For the model shown, turn the piece to a diameter of 2½ inches. Then use a parting tool to cut a ⅜-inch-square groove around the stock, ⅜ inch from the headstock-end. The groove will accommodate the split rings of the chuck. Remove the blank from the lathe, slide the threaded collar over the blank, and insert the split rings into the groove, ensuring the sloping faces of the rings face toward the collar (top). Assemble the chuck by placing the center

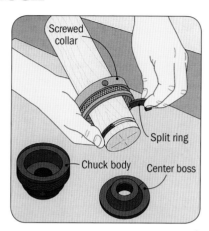

boss against the threaded collar with the tapered end facing out, then screw the chuck body to the threaded collar (bottom). Tighten the unit using the wrenches supplied with the chuck. This will lock the blank in place. Finally, screw the assembly onto the lathe's headstock spindle.

COLLET CHUCK

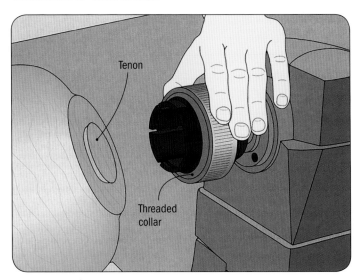

Once you have shaped the outside of your blank, a collet chuck will enable you to attach the bottom to the headstock of the lathe for hollowing out the inside. This chuck is similar in operation to the contracting-jaw scroll chuck described on page 120. To prepare a blank for the chuck, turn a dovetailed tenon on the bottom. (Follow the manufacturer's instructions for the appropriate size of the tenon.) For the model shown, the tenon should be slightly smaller in diameter than the chuck's collet when it is opened. (You may remove the tenon once the inside of the bowl is turned.) Next, install the chuck on the headstock spindle, insert the tenon in the collet, and tighten the threaded collar—first by hand, then using the wrenches supplied with the chuck.

COLLAR CHUCK

The collar chuck allows you to secure goblets and other long blanks on the lathe's headstock without using the tailstock. Prepare your stock and assemble the chuck following the manufacturer's instructions. For the model shown, start by mounting

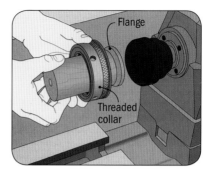

Flange

Threaded collar

it between centers, then turn it into a cylinder with a diameter of 2½ inches, with a ½-inch-long sloping flange, or collar, at the headstock end of the workpiece. The diameter of the flange should be at least 2¾ inches. Once the blank is ready, remove it from the lathe and slide the threaded collar onto it, making certain the sloping face of the flange faces the collar (above). Finally, tighten the collar on the chuck body using the wrenches provided with the chuck.

Jacobs Chuck

Although the Jacobs chuck, like the one shown in the photo below, is normally used in the tailstock to hold drill bits for hollowing, it is also ideal for securing small-diameter blanks to the headstock. Here, the chuck holds a chess piece made of tulipwood.

CHAPTER 9:

Bowl Turning

There is no single way to turn a bowl. As you gain experience faceplate turning, you will develop a technique that works best for you and the work you do. The techniques shown in these pages provide a starting point for further experimentation.

The bowl gouge is the workhorse of bowl turning. As shown on page 131, you must always try to keep the gouge's bevel rubbing lightly on the blank as it cuts. This will provide support for the cutting edge and control the depth of cut. Depending on the shape of your blank, this may be difficult to do as you start to turn a bowl. In this case, set the lathe to its lowest speed until you have rounded the blank to a disk. A gouge cuts most smoothly when the cutting edge is slightly over on its side so the flute faces the direction of the cut.

Scraping tools are also used extensively in bowl turning. For roughing out waste, the blade must lie flat on the tool rest.

The direction of cut is also critical. Because the grain of faceplate work runs at a right angle to the lathe axis, your cutting will run against the grain as well as with it. As much as possible when turning the outside of a bowl, cuts should run from small diameter to large, or from the bottom of the bowl to the top. Inside work should be performed moving the tool in the other direction, from the rim to the bottom.

BODY AND TOOL POSITION

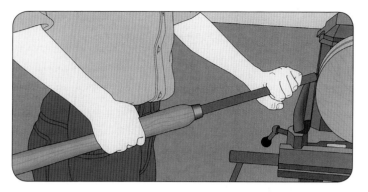

Stand close to the lathe, with your feet a comfortable distance apart. Grasp the tool in both hands: Hold the middle of the handle with your right hand; with your left hand, grip the blade near the tip and press it down firmly on the tool rest. Holding the tool midway on the handle makes it easy to move the cutting edge. Tool movements are generated by shifting your body in a controlled manner. Moving your arms and hands alone tends to make the tool swing in an arc and reduces your control over the cut.

TOOL BASICS

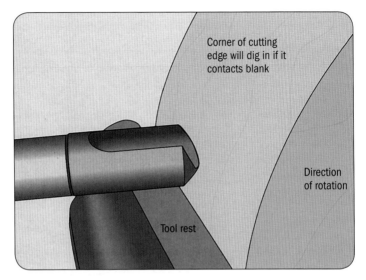

Corner of cutting edge will dig in if it contacts blank

Direction of rotation

Tool rest

Incorrect

Touching a bowl gouge to a spinning blank without the bevel rubbing (above) is dangerous for you and damaging for your workpiece. With the cutting edge in this position, the cut is virtually impossible to control. You run the risk of digging the cutting edge into the piece. This can produce unsightly notches in your stock and cause you to lose control of the tool. Another mistake is pushing the cutting edge against the wood before the tool contacts the tool rest. This will invariably slam the blade against the tool rest with a force that could damage the work, the tool rest, or the gouge.

TOOL BASICS *(continued)*

Correct

Brace the blade on the tool rest before it contacts the wood. Then, with the handle held low, advance the tool toward the spinning blank until the heel of the bevel is rubbing against the wood (top right). To begin cutting, gradually lift the handle, bringing the cutting edge in contact with the stock and the bevel flush against the wood (bottom right). Keep in mind that the tool will travel in the direction that the flute is pointed.

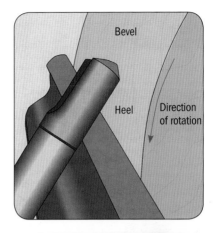

Bevel

Heel

Direction of rotation

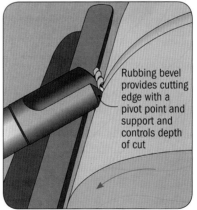

Rubbing bevel provides cutting edge with a pivot point and support and controls depth of cut

Tool Basics

ROUNDING THE BLANK

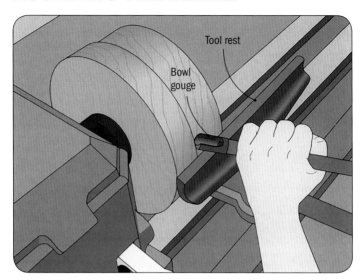

Tool rest

Bowl gouge

Mount the blank on the lathe headstock and position the tool rest ¼ inch from the stock. Rotate the blank by hand to ensure that it does not contact the rest, then turn on the lathe. Bracing the gouge on the tool rest at one edge of the piece, advance the blade until the heel of the bevel contacts the stock. Then pivot up the handle until the cutting edge begins slicing into the wood. Roll the gouge so that the flute is facing the direction of the cut—in this case, toward the headstock-end of the lathe—and move the tool along the blank to remove a thin layer of wood (above). Continue in this manner until the diameter of the blank is slightly greater than the finished bowl diameter. Once the shape is satisfactory and the bowl is the proper diameter, flatten the base (page 135) before shaping the outside.

SHAPING THE OUTSIDE

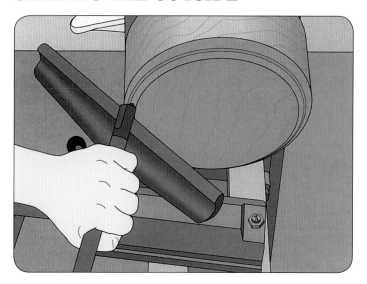

Position the tool rest ¼ inch from the corner of the blank and angled at roughly 45° to the bottom. Adjust the height of the rest so it is level with the center of the blank. Set the gouge on the right-hand side of the tool rest with the flute pointing in the direction of the cut. Starting on the bottom of the bowl about 1 inch from the corner of the blank, advance the tool until the bevel rubs on the stock.

Pivot the tool handle up until the edge is cutting, then move the tool to the left to chamfer the corner (above). Continue, cutting from the center outward to the edges to round the corner of the blank. Move the tool rest periodically to keep it as close as possible to the blank.

ROUNDING THE OUTSIDE

Continue working from the center toward the rim of the blank (from smaller to larger diameter) to shape the outside of the bowl to the desired diameter and curve. Reposition the tool rest as necessary to follow the curve of the bowl. Always brace the gouge on the tool rest,

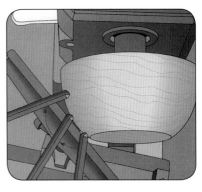

making certain the flute faces the direction of the cut—from the bottom to the top of the bowl. As shown at right, you will need to pivot the handle and roll the blade to keep the bevel rubbing on the stock.

Final Shaping

Refine the shape of the bowl with the bowl gouge, adding design elements such as concave curves or decorative grooves at this time. Keep the flute pointing in the direction of the cut and the bevel rubbing on the wood (right). Remember to account for the

method you will use to chuck the bottom of the bowl to the headstock to hollow out the inside. If you will be turning a dovetailed recess for an expanding jaw chuck (page 121), as on the blank shown, leave the bottom flat and large enough for the recess.

FLATTENING THE BOTTOM

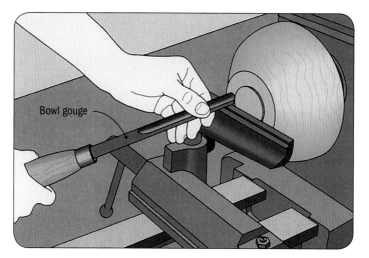

Bowl gouge

Once you have shaped the outside of the bowl, it is time to reverse the blank by attaching the base to the lathe head-stock so you can hollow out the vessel. If using a glue block, first flatten the base with a bowl gouge or square-end scraper. If you will be using a chuck, you can prepare the base of the bowl for it (page 121). To flatten the base, position the tool rest parallel to the base. Tilt the gouge's handle down a little and cut from the outside toward the center (above), removing wood in thin layers until the base is flat. If you are using a scraper, angle the handle up slightly so the burr on the cutting edge is shaving wood from the base (right). Periodically use a straightedge, such as a rule, to check whether the bottom is flat. Hold the rule on edge against the base and look for any gaps.

Square-end scraper

CUTTING CHUCK RECESS

Fitting the Chuck

If you will be using a chuck that calls for a dovetailed recess in the base, as on the bowl illustrated on this page, use a side-cutting skew scraper to form the recess. The cavity should be sized to fit the jaws of the chuck; you can use dividers to mark the required diameter on the

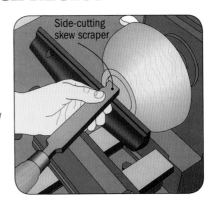

base. Then position the tool rest slightly below the center of the base so that the scraper's edge will lie at the centerline. Hold the scraper blade flat on the rest and, with the handle lifted up slightly, advance the tool to the left of the center until the burr contacts the blank. Cut the recess slowly to the depth specified by the chuck manufacturer. Then slide the scraper to the edge of the cavity and cut the dovetail in the wall of the recess (top). Keep the blade flat on the tool rest throughout the operation.

When you have completed the recess, assemble the jaws of the chuck, using an elastic band to hold them together, and fit the jaws in place to check the fit (right). The jaws should go all the way in with a small amount of clearance. Deepen or widen the recess if necessary.

SMOOTHING THE OUTSIDE

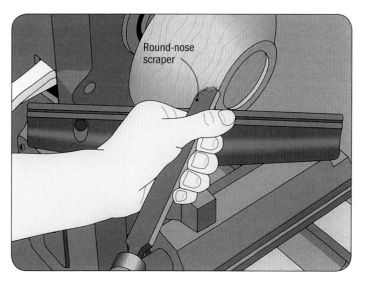

Round-nose scraper

Although a gouge leaves the outside of the bowl relatively uniform, it may also leave a few ripples. Dragging a scraper very lightly across the surface will clean up the surface. This operation is known as "shear scraping." Position the tool rest parallel to the outside of the bowl and turn on the lathe. Hold a freshly sharpened round-nosed scraper with one corner of the blade contacting the tool rest, as shown at right. Starting at the bottom of the bowl, drag the cutting edge lightly and smoothly along the outside of the bowl, working from the base toward the rim. The cut should produce fine shavings. Repeat the cut as often as necessary until you produce the finish you want.

SANDING THE OUTSIDE

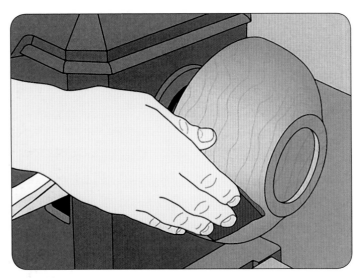

The final step before hollowing out the inside of a bowl is sanding the outside. You can either work by hand or use a random-orbit sander. In either case, move the lathe's tool rest out of the way. If you are working by hand, fold the sandpaper twice, turn on the lathe, and hold the paper lightly against the blank. Keep the paper below the middle of the bowl (top) and move the pad from the base to the rim of the bowl to cover the entire surface. With the power sander, work the same way, holding the sanding disk lightly against the surface (bottom). Start with 100-grit paper and move to progressively finer grits.

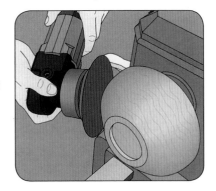

HOLLOWING THE INSIDE

Once you have turned the outside of a bowl, it is time to hollow it out. The shape of a bowl's inside should complement the outside. A bowl can have attractive outside and inside forms, but if the surfaces do not harmonize, the finished piece will not look right. As a novice bowl turner, you should aim for walls of uniform thickness. For small- to medium-sized bowls, ⅛-to ¼-inch-thick walls work well. As you gain experience, do not hesitate to experiment.

The most important rule when hollowing out is to cut toward the axis of the lathe—that is, from large to small diameter. The advantage of this approach is your cuts will run with the grain, giving you better control of the tool and producing a cleaner surface.

Once you are ready to hollow out the interior, chuck the bowl base to the headstock using one of the methods described earlier in the chapter. Then flatten the face of the mouth, as shown in the photo below. To prevent the rim from splintering, touch it lightly with a bowl gouge to round it over slightly. Now you are ready to rough out the inside. Once you have removed the bulk of the waste and the inside of the bowl has the rough form you want, use a scraper to refine the surface.

A crucial step before hollowing out the inside of a bowl is to flatten the face of the mouth. This will ensure that the distance between the rim and the base is uniform all around the circumference.

HOLLOWING THE INSIDE *(continued)*

Making a Depth Hole

One way to make certain you hollow a bowl to the correct depth is to drill a hole into the mouth to the desired depth. With the blank mounted on the lathe, install a Jacobs chuck and a twist or brad-point bit in the tailstock. Mark the desired depth on the bit with a piece of masking tape, then turn on the lathe. Slide the tailstock toward the blank until the bit starts cutting. Advance the tailstock until the masking tape contacts the blank.

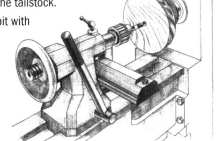

Measuring Depth

Before you begin hollowing the bowl, measure the depth of the blank to determine how far you can cut into the mouth before you will reach the chuck recess or faceplate screws. Holding a rule directly above the blank, measure from the mouth to the base. The bowl shown in the illustration is secured to the lathe headstock with a chuck. Subtract the depth of the recess for the chuck (in this case, ¼ inch) and the eventual thickness of the base (about ¼ inch) to arrive at the depth to which you can cut (for the bowl shown, 2¼ inches).

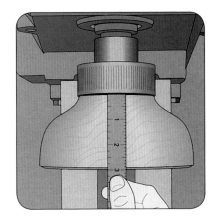

HOLLOWING THE INSIDE *(continued)*

Position the tool rest so the gouge tip cuts slightly above the middle of the blank. Turn on the lathe and align the cutting edge just to the left of the center of the blank. Then, with the gouge on its side and the flute facing the center of the piece, push the tool slowly into the blank. For the first ⅛ inch, the bevel will not be rubbing against the wood. Once it begins to rub, guide the cutting edge to the center of the blank. Continue the process, forming a shallow cavity in the middle of the mouth. As the cavity becomes larger, pivot the handle from side to side in a shallow arc, as shown above, pushing the cutting edge against the side of the hole until it reaches the center. (The hands have been removed from the illustration for clarity.) Support the blade as you would to shape the outside (page 133). Turn the inside of the bowl to match the outside, but leave the walls a little thicker than you need. You will

reach your final thickness as you smooth and scrape the inside. As you approach your final depth, it may be difficult to make one fluid cut along the inside wall of the bowl. If so, you can make a series of shorter cuts from the rim to the center.

Finishing the inside

As the depth of bowl increases, you need to angle the tool rest so it
remains roughly parallel to the surface you are cutting. Or, you can turn
off the lathe, remove the standard tool rest, and install an S-shaped rest.
Position it so that part of the S is inside the bowl and roughly follows its
curvature. Turn on the lathe again. Starting at the rim, make a light cut
to trim the walls to the desired thickness. With the gouge pivoted well to
the right, advance the tool into the cut and swing the handle to the left,
keeping the bevel rubbing at all times. This technique yields a smooth
curve on the inside of the bowl. To obtain uniform wall thickness from the
rim to the bottom, keep the bevel aligned with the outside profile of the
bowl throughout the cut. Adjust the tool rest to keep it as close as possible
to the inside surface of the bowl. Periodically measure wall thickness.

HOLLOWING THE INSIDE *(continued)*

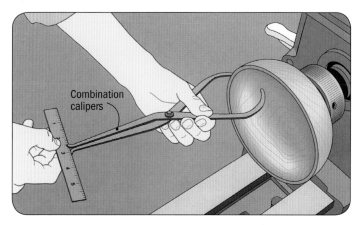

Combination calipers

Checking Thickness

At the start of the hollowing out process, you can gauge the wall thickness with your hands. But as you approach your final thickness, use combination calipers for a more precise reading. Close one end of the calipers around the bowl near the top and bottom and measure the opening at the other end to determine the thickness of the wall (above). Continue finishing the inside until the thickness is uniform.

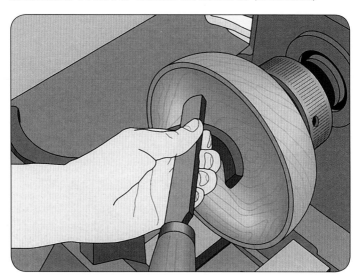

Scraping

Use a round-nosed scraper to shear-scrape the inside of the bowl before sanding. To avoid digging the blade into the wood, the curvature of the cutting edge must be tighter than the curve of the bowl's interior. Adjust the S-shaped tool rest so it roughly follows the inside of the bowl. Then, raising the scraper handle so the burr is even with the center of the bowl, press the scraper lightly against the inside of the bowl. With the blade at a 45° angle to the axis of the bowl, drag the blade gently over the entire interior surface, working from the bottom of the bowl to the rim until you obtain the desired smoothness (above).

HOLLOWING THE INSIDE *(continued)*

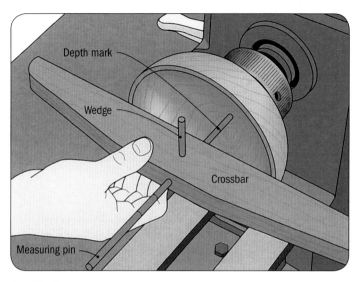

Depth Gauge

Use the shop-made gauge shown below to check the depth of your bowl as you hollow it out. The jig is easy to build from scrap wood and ¼-inch dowel. Make the crossbar two or three times longer than the diameter of the largest bowl you can turn on your lathe. Cut it to the shape shown for a convenient grip.

To insert the measuring pin and wedge dowels, bore one hole from edge to edge through the middle of the crossbar and a second hole through from the top. The wedge hole should overlap the pin hole slightly so the wedge will hold the pin in place. Drill both holes with a ¼-inch bit. Cut a long dowel for the measuring pin and round over its bowl-end with sandpaper to prevent the tip from scratching the inside of the bowl. Mark depth intervals on the pin using a ruler and a pencil. Next, cut a shorter dowel for the wedge and taper its bottom end.

HOLLOWING THE INSIDE *(continued)*

Hand Sanding

Fold a piece of 100-grit sandpaper and move the lathe's tool rest out of the way. Turn on the lathe, and hold the paper lightly against the inside surface of the bowl. Keep the paper below the mid-line of the bowl (right) and

move the pad from the bottom to the rim to smooth the entire surface. Continue the process with a series of finer-grit papers.

Power Sanding

You can also use an electric drill fitted with an accessory sanding disk to smooth the inside of the bowl. Work the same way as you would with sandpaper, holding the sanding disk lightly against the surface (right).

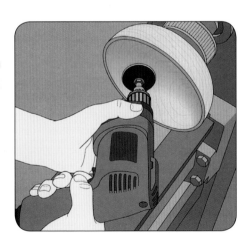

FINISHING

With the bowl still on the lathe, saturate a rag or sponge with tung oil (varnish or lacquer may also be used), or a food-safe finish if the bowl will hold food, and run the machine at its slowest speed. Starting with the outside of the bowl, hold the rag lightly against the surface (above), moving from the base to the rim. Use a clean, dry, lint-free rag to wipe off any excess finish. Then saturate the rag again and apply another coat to the inside of the bowl. Once the finish has dried, sand the bowl with 400-grit paper and wipe it clean. Apply several coats the same way, sanding between applications. With more coats, the bowl will better resist cracking and damage from heat and water.

Once a bowl is turned and sanded smooth, a finish can be applied. Because the bowl shown here is intended to hold food, it is given a light coating of mineral oil with a lint-free cotton pad.

147

Index

Back to **Basics**

Straight Talk for Today's **Woodworker**

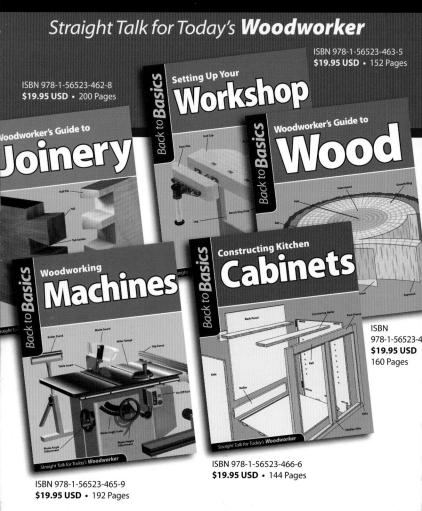

ISBN 978-1-56523-463-5
$19.95 USD • 152 Pages

ISBN 978-1-56523-462-8
$19.95 USD • 200 Pages

Back to **Basics** — Setting Up Your **Workshop**

Woodworker's Guide to **Joinery**

Woodworker's Guide to **Wood**

Woodworking **Machines**

Constructing Kitchen **Cabinets**

ISBN
978-1-56523-4
$19.95 USD
160 Pages

ISBN 978-1-56523-466-6
$19.95 USD • 144 Pages

ISBN 978-1-56523-465-9
$19.95 USD • 192 Pages

Get *Back to Basics* with the core information you need to succeed. This new series offers a clear road map of fundamental woodworking knowledge on sixteen essential topics. It explains what's important to know now and what can be left for later. Best of all, it's presented in the plain-spoken language you'd hear from a trusted friend or relative. The world's already complicated—your woodworking information shouldn't be.

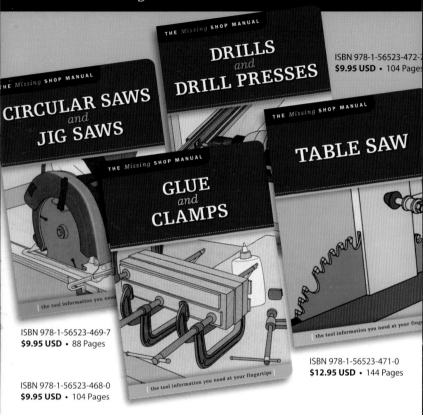